NATURAL STYLE

NATURAL STYLE

Decorating approaches for
a pure, simple home

LINDSAY PORTER

LORENZ BOOKS

This edition first published in 1998 by Lorenz Books
27 West 20th Street, New York, NY 10011

LORENZ BOOKS are available for bulk purchase for sales promotion and for
premium use. For details write or call the manager of special sales:
Lorenz Books, 27 West 20th Street
New York, NY 10011; (800) 354-9657

Lorenz Books is an imprint of Anness Publishing Limited

ISBN 1 85967 592 1

Publisher: Joanna Lorenz
Senior Editor: Lindsay Porter
Text editor: Judith Casey
Designer: Bobbie Colgate Stone

Printed and bound in Hong Kong

10 9 8 7 6 5 4 3 2 1

Contents

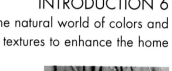

INTRODUCTION

"When we see a natural style, we are quite surprised
and delighted"

BLAISE PASCAL

Purely natural

Crisp cotton, soft wool, heavy linen, smooth wood, cool stone, textural rush matting: these are the ingredients of the natural home. They have an enduring quality because they come from nature; their appeal is universal because we all understand them and they simply can't go out of fashion. Natural materials age exquisitely. Just compare a pine floor, bright and new, with one that has mellowed to a golden patina over time. Think of wonderful crisp linen sheets; then compare them to those that have been laundered and pressed time and again for an altogether softer, more fluid fabric.

This book uses natural materials as its starting point and nature for its inspiration. True to its origins, natural style is unfussy; it prefers simplicity for a clear, uncluttered and harmonious look. However, natural style does not prescribe. It does not dictate certain colours or particular furniture designs. Natural style is more about finding your own style; about mixing but not

necessarily matching; about using simple tricks to link what could seem disparate pieces of furniture or accessories. Half a dozen old kitchen chairs, picked up from junk shops, can be co-ordinated with a lick of paint and perhaps a simple, tie-on cushion. White or cream china, old or new, always looks good, even if the pieces come from different eras.

So how do you go about finding your own style? How do you create a beautiful, tranquil home? The

simple

understated

tactile

unique

key is simplicity. Start with a simple canvas – that is the walls, floors and window treatments. Try to keep the whole "canvas" tonal, avoiding hard contrasts, which can be distracting. Even architectural details, such as skirting (base) boards and architraves can have the effect of carving up the room depending on the colour you choose. Pick them out, if you want, but choose a tone that offers a soft contrast to the walls. When choosing colours of finishes for walls and floors, think of your home as a whole rather than as a series of rooms. The aim is to bring harmony and cohesion. This can be achieved by choosing a limited palette and working within that – add interest to interconnecting rooms with different finishes: stamps, textured plaster or even crackle-glaze on the woodwork.

Choices of furniture and lighting, fabrics and accessories are set against this simple, basic canvas. The key here is proportion. Pieces that are too small for a room can become lost, while those that are too large become overbearing. Next, look for balance: check that your items are neither too heavy nor too spindly for their height; that they look good from every angle. Look for items with good basic designs; you will then be free to change the finish as you desire. You can completely change the character of a chair, for example, depending on whether you paint it, gild it, wrap it with rope, or simply cover it with a

favourite throw.

This is the idea behind natural style: creating an uncluttered home that makes the most of natural materials and timelessly classic shapes. Leaf through the pages of this book for a treasury of ideas that show you how to make it work within the framework of your own home.

White

"Lawn as white as driven snow"
WILLIAM SHAKESPEARE

White symbolizes purity, innocence and honesty. Found naturally in snow and flowers, white comes in many shades from creamy yellows to cool blue tints. Cream and off-white have always been popular for decorating, whereas the brightest of white paint was not used until the 20th century.

White is also the colour for freshness and cleanliness. Imagine a bed made with crisp white cotton sheets or a bathroom filled with fluffy white towels. Simple yet luxurious. Add lace and broderie anglaise (eyelet lace) to plain sheeting to make it extra special.

It's also a good colour for unifying a mismatched collection, such as china and napkins. A setting of white

Above: The all-white arrangement on this box lid emphasizes the natural sculputural quality of the shells.

Above: Whites and naturals in the bathroom.

eggshell

porcelain

swansdown

milk

Above: Airy and cool – white cotton lace at the window.

china can look plain and simple or grand and formal, depending on the cutlery and table-linen you choose. Add a selection of plain white candles for the evening. Paint chairs in white or off-white to create a co-ordinating set.

White is the perfect foil for stronger colours, such as black, red and all shades of blue. Think of fresh, crisp gingham and pinstriped fabrics, as examples of white-and-colour combinations.

Muslin, voile, broderie anglaise and cotton sheeting are all inexpensive sources of white fabrics. Use them generously as floor-length tablecloths, for covering chairs and to make long, floaty curtains. Combine white fabrics with textured materials such as wood or metal for strong contrast.

Above: Accents of colour can be used to punctuate an all-white theme.

Left: Pure white candles, crockery and flowers create an effortlessly beautiful table setting.

Blue

"Blue, darkly, deeply, beautifully blue"
ROBERT SOUTHEY

Blue symbolizes hope and sincerity and is a restful colour to live with. It is sometimes thought of as cold, but blue comes in many shades from cool turquoise to bright cornflower. Think of an unclouded sky, the sea, or a curling drift of woodsmoke to imagine the range of tones. The stronger shades of cornflower and periwinkle are lovely warm colours, perfect for cool kitchens and bathrooms.

Team blue and white for a classic combination. Found in crisp nautical themes and floral-patterned china, blue and white can give a clean, graphic look or a pretty, soft impression.

Blue and yellow is a fresh combination, evoking sea and sand. Perfect for bedrooms, it's a combination that looks good in a bathroom too.

Above: A fresh blue-and-white scheme for the bathroom.

azure

cornflower

midnight

kingfisher

Right: Denim, a classic blue.

The expression "blue and green should never be seen", has been re-evaluated in recent years. Blue-green is a popular Mediterranean shade that's easy to live with. Paint furniture with a layer of green, rub with wax, then paint over with blue for a contemporary distressed look.

Grow delphiniums, cornflowers, lavender and blue-bells for their vibrant shades of blue. Pick fresh lavender heads in the early morning for drying, and you can enjoy their heady scent all year round.

Left: Think ice-blue for cool interiors.

Above: Blue colourwashed floorboards evoke beach huts.

Left: Bright blue paint transforms an old wicker chair.

Above: Strong blues combined with natural shades always work well, whether for a small arrangement or an entire room.

Green

"Of green days in forests and blue days at sea"
ROBERT LOUIS STEVENSON

Green is a restful colour to live with, symbolizing nature, new growth and freshness. From cool mint to dusky sage, zingy lime to strong emerald, there are many shades found in nature. As with nature's leaves and bark, all shades of green tone well with wood. It's the perfect colour for creating a garden-room atmosphere. Decorate the room in creams and whites and fill with an abundance of lush green plants.

Soft sage or moss green are good neutral background colours for carpets and sofas, whereas a brighter tone such as lime is good as an accent colour. Add touches of bright green to a room by arranging green bottles on a windowsill to catch the light.

Top, above and right: Draw inspiration from the many shades of green that occur in nature – from zesty lime to deep leaf green.

Historically, subtle greens were thought most suitable for bedrooms because of their calming effect, but they are now popular for other rooms as well. In recent years, deep saturated greens have become popular for kitchens and bathrooms.

Green is also a good mixer, contrasting well with yellow, blue, pink and white. Make sure you select the right shade, keeping bright tones together and subtle shades together. For example, soft sage green contrasts well with dusty pink, but would be overshadowed by a strong fuschia shade.

emerald

lime

sage

moss

Right, from top: Work within one colour range when choosing shades: mint green, jade green or bottle green.

Left: Acid green can be combined with citrus shades.

Below: Bright spring green is fresh with white.

15

Red

"O, my Luve's like a red red rose"
ROBERT BURNS

Ranging from pale pink to deep crimson, red comes in a range of tones. Red is a strong colour that adds warmth and grandeur to any room. It can be teamed with white and gold for a formal effect. It's particularly good in dining rooms, where it creates a warm, intimate atmosphere in the evening.

Red also suggests romance – red roses, hearts and wine. Add touches of red to rooms and accessories, by

Above: Use a strong colour sparingly for maximum impact. Berry-red bath beads and soap are off-set by cool grey-blues.

Above and below right: Nature provides many examples of pure, deep, saturated reds.

way of ribbons, stencils and cushions, to add definition to neutral schemes.

Red adds warmth to north-facing rooms. Instead of painting a small room in white, you could aim to emphasize its cosiness by painting the walls in deep red. Contrast the walls with natural coir matting and a few strong accessories.

Choose red and white in combination for a kitchen with a French feel. Fresh gingham curtains and a table-cloth look good day and night for lunches and informal suppers. Team gingham with white china and chunky wine glasses to carry through the country theme.

Choose red roses, tulips and red hot pokers for hot spots in the garden. Create a hot border in the sun to bring the Mediterranean to your doorstep.

flame

wine

rose

vermilion

Above: A simple yet stunning arrangement of single flowerheads in toning shades.

Above: Mix patterned fabric in the same shade of red.

Right: An antique shirt made of red lawn is a decorative feature in its own right.

Yellow

"Come unto these yellow sands"
WILLIAM SHAKESPEARE

Yellow is a happy colour suggesting sunshine and warmth. In heraldry it signifies faith, constancy, wisdom and glory. It was a popular colour in the 18th century and is in vogue again with the interest in Mediterranean shades. Ranging from golden corn to pale primrose, yellow is a warm colour that's easy to live with and seems to lift the spirits.

Visit France in the summer and you will see field after field of golden sunflowers. Just a few of these dried sunflowers in an earthenware vase will bring a touch of Provence to your kitchen and will last all year round. A bowl of lemons on a kitchen table would also bring a splash of colour.

sunflower

saffron

maize

buttercup

Above: Perhaps the most evocative yellow of them all – the rich, warm shade of sunflower petals.

Left: Creamy yellow beeswax candles will add a warm glow to dark winter's evenings.

Pale yellow painted walls look good combined with green, blue or grey accessories for a cool theme. Alternatively, turn up the heat by using spicy Indian colours such as yellow ochre, rust and pink – think of the warm colours found in Madras checked fabrics.

Yellow also suggests springtime, when daffodils, primroses and forsythia are in full bloom. Gather bunches of flowers to bring indoors and celebrate the arrival of the warmer weather. Pick some stems of pale yellow catkin and arrange them in a terracotta pot – a splash of yellow will immediately evoke sunshine indoors.

Left: Consider all shades of yellow when devising room schemes.

Above: An all-yellow theme creates a light and sunny impression.

Left and right: Lemon yellow is refreshing and guaranteed to lift the spirits.

Wood

"Under the greenwood tree
Who loves to lie with me"
WILLIAM SHAKESPEARE

Wood is a natural and versatile material. It is strong and beautiful, and comes in many shades from pale cream pine to deep red mahogany. You can change its look by finishing it with paint, wax or varnish according to the style you want to achieve.

Old wood, full of imperfections, has a wonderful feel to it. It needn't be costly either; driftwood, wooden pallets and old doors from salvage yards are all inexpensive, and making new items out of old wood gives them immediate character. The patina of age on old wooden furniture is particularly special - do not be tempted to "clean it up" by stripping the surface, otherwise this natural "veneer" will be lost.

Above: Colour gives way to texture in this simple arrangement.

Different woods complement each other. For example, old pine has the same honey colour as natural beech. Paler woods include oak, ash and Scandinavian pine. Dark woods such as old oak and mahogany have a more formal look.

Add your own paint effects to wooden furniture to add individuality. Stamping, distressing, liming and stencilling are all ideal. Decoupage is good too, finished with a coat of varnish to protect the paper cut-outs.

Above: A frame makes the most of the distressed quality of the wood.

Left: The strong vertical lines of the bamboo canes forming this plant holder are echoed in the scallop shell decoration.

Right: The natural beauty of twigs has been retained in these containers.

oak

ash

beech

willow

Above: A rustic basket made of twigs.

Above: A twig tray embellished with natural raffia.

Above: Use unfinished wood for decorative detail.

Right: A twig screen – for use inside the home – recalls traditional fencing in the countryside.

Metal

"Here's metal more attractive"
WILLIAM SHAKESPEARE

Hard and shiny, metal has become a popular decorative material in recent years. Apart from the traditional silver picture frames and pewter tankards, you'll now find stainless steel, copper and punched tin home accessories, and a wealth of items made from wire, including candelabras, egg holders and lampshades.

Above and below: The matt texture of galvanized tin has a raw, unfinished beauty.

As well as forming the main structure, wire is also used for adding decoration. Panels of humble chicken wire stretched behind cupboard doors give a rustic, country look to a kitchen. Leave the panels unlined, so you can see the contents of the cupboard, or back them with fresh checked fabric. You can remove lids and labels from food cans to make a collection of inexpensive storage pots.

Chunky wrought-iron candlesticks are also very popular. Wrought-iron has a heavy, handmade feel about it

that suits today's simple, pared-down decorating style.

Galvanized metal has come in from the garden, so milk churns, florists' buckets and watering cans are now used decoratively in the home as vases, umbrella stands and wastebaskets.

Don't be put off by the thought of metal being a hard craft material to work with. Tin is a soft metal, and wire is easy to bend into shape. Wear the proper protective clothing and, with a bit of practice, you will discover a versatile and reasonably inexpensive material to work with.

Above: Combine shiny and matt metal pieces.

tin

copper

steel

iron

Above, below and left: Gleaming utensils and buckets, with or without punched embellishments, make great focal points.

23

Glass

"Life, like a dome of many-coloured glass"
PERCY SHELLEY

It is the reflective quality of glass that makes it special. Clear or coloured, plain or painted, glassware comes in many guises. A collection of old and new bottles in toning colours makes a simple but effective window display, catching the light like stained glass. If you can't display your glass collection in front of a window, arrange it on a shelf and devise lighting either above or below to set it off.

Clear glass tumblers and bottles with a good shape are perfect as candleholders. Fill them with white candles of different heights and thicknesses, and arrange them on a side-table at Christmas time.

Painting on glass is very popular and a good way of recycling attractively shaped bottles. There are special glass paints available that do not need firing and that come in a wide range of translucent colours. Draw your design on to the bottle with outliner, then fill in the areas with coloured paints and leave to dry.

Natural style glass calls for strong shapes rather than intricate engraving or extravagant facets. Look for chunky drinking vessels made from recycled glass, either plain or in strong colours. Seconds, available from factory shops, have blips and air bubbles in them, making each glass slightly different.

Right and opposite: A collection of antique bottles positioned on a windowsill will catch the light or may be used to display single flower heads.

Above: Float candles and flower heads in a glass bowl for a striking centrepiece.

24

crystal

clear

coloured

stained

Above and right: Strong, simple shapes in clear glass are design classics and best suited to the natural home.

Stone

"Quiet as a stone"

JOHN KEATS

Smooth and hard, stone is perhaps an unusual decorative material for the home. You may be lucky enough to have a stone fire surround in your living room, but most often stone will be confined to accessories. Because of its weight, stone is used for making small items, such as bookends or paperweights.

Smooth, round pebbles from the seaside are naturally beautiful. Roll one around in your hand and feel its weight. Unfortunately, it is now illegal to remove large stones from the beach, but you can buy them from garden centres and authorized traders. Arrange two or three coloured pebbles on the hearth.

flint

marble

slate

granite

Above: Stones with intricate hand-painted patterns.

Below: Beautiful vessels made from drilled stones.

Left: Practical yet with an understated decorative effect, pebbles are used to weigh down a tablecloth for outdoor eating.

Left: A pair of pots with a chunky "earthy" quality.

Garden centres are a great source of stone pots and ornaments to bring indoors. Their weight and size gives them great impact and they can look good in traditional or modern settings. For example a stone bench would make an imposing seat in an entrance hall. Choose four matching stone ornaments and rest a heavy sheet of glass on top to make an unusual coffee table. Have the edges of the glass smoothed and rounded by a glazier, and protect it with felt pads. Do ensure your floors can cope with particularly heavy items.

Above: Slates of marble off-set a plaster shell.

Above: A distressed terracotta jug is complemented by the plaster wall behind.

Right: Chips of stone and marble mosaic decorate the front of a step.

Natural Cloth

"In blanched linen, smooth and lavender'd"
JOHN KEATS

Nowadays people are moving away from mass-produced goods in favour of handmade and natural things. Natural fabrics such as linen, hessian (burlap) and muslin are used more and more as furnishing fabrics. The weave can be slightly uneven which gives them added texture and interest. Use generous lengths of fabric to create curtains, tablecloths and bedcovers.

Cotton has always been popular for soft furnishings because it is hardwearing and washable and it comes in a wide variety of weights from strong calico and ticking, to checked gingham and fine lawn. Wool, although not as hardwearing as cotton, is warm and welcoming in the home. Dress a sofa with a woollen throw and piles of knitted cushions in toning colours.

Above: String – one of the humblest of materials – has a natural simplicity.

Raffia and string have become popular to use as decorative trimmings such as curtain tiebacks and shelf edging. Look in your local garden centre for sources of inspiration. As well as their natural shade, raffia and string come in a selection of colours, or you can dye them yourself to match your chosen colour scheme. Knit up balls of natural string into knobbly cushions, and trim them with wooden buttons, or simply twist string around napkins or vases for a simple decoration.

Left: Linen napkins in neutral shades tied with complementary raffia tassels.

linen
cotton
muslin
wool

Left: Builder's scrim is woven to make a light-diffusing screen for the window.

Below: A natural string tassel decorates a utilitarian deck chair.

Above and right: Natural linen is hard-wearing, versatile and beautiful in the home.

FABRICS

"No perfumes but very fine linen, plenty of it,

and country washing"

BEAU BRUMMEL

Introduction

"Delicate-filmed as new-spun silk"
THOMAS HARDY

Natural fabrics are wonderfully tactile. Think of cotton, canvas, hessian (burlap), linen, muslin and voile, and you can describe them by the way they feel — smooth or rough, soft or silky. Fabrics made from natural fibres have timeless appeal. Many fabrics — such as denim — seem actually to improve with age. Choose them undyed, plain white or, at most, with simple stripes, and they will blend together beautifully to give your home understated elegance and style.

Above: Mixing and matching checks in similar colors is a quick way of refreshing a tired or worn-out bedroom scheme.

Left: Lengths of inexpensive muslin were used to create a bed canopy.

lacey bedlinen

muslin curtains

linen tablecloths

silky throws

Use fabrics generously when making curtains, chair covers and bedspreads for maximum drama. Add natural touches to soft furnishings by way of shells and string, or raid your sewing basket for small pieces of lace, embroidery thread and trimmings.

Right: Crisp, white bedlinen remains a popular choice. Consider edging new sheets with lenghts of antique lace.

Above: Understated comfort is provided by natural fabrics in neutral shades, embellished with yachting rope and chrome eyelets.

STRINGWORK CURTAINS

Ordinary white cotton string is excellent for large-scale furnishing projects such as these full-length curtains. The appealing, child-like design of large daisies is appliquéd directly on to the plain background fabric. For a child's room you could stitch the white flowers on to a bright-coloured fabric.

YOU WILL NEED
linen or linen-like fabric
tape measure
scissors
iron
dressmaker's pins
needle and tacking (basting) thread
matching sewing thread
sewing machine (optional)
dressmaker's pencil
white cotton string
white sewing thread

1 Decide on the size of the finished curtains. Add 5 cm/2 in to the width and 9 cm/3½ in to the length and cut out the fabric. Fold in 1 cm/½ in along the long sides of the fabric and iron. Fold over another 1.5 cm/⅝ in. Pin, tack (baste) and stitch the hems, then iron. Measure the width of the curtains and decide how many tabs are needed, assuming that the tabs will be 5.5 cm/2¾ in wide with 9 cm/3½ in gaps between them.

2 Multiply the number of tabs by 24 cm/9½ in; cut a strip of fabric to this length and 17 cm/6½ in wide. Fold the strip of fabric in half lengthways. Pin, tack and stitch along the long edge with right sides together, leaving a 1 cm/½ in seam allowance. Press the seams open. Turn the tubes the right way out and iron flat with the seam positioned centrally on one side of the tube. Cut the strip into 24 cm/9½ in lengths. Tuck 1 cm/½ in inside at each end. Pin, tack and stitch in place.

3 Fold in 1 cm/½ in along the top edge of the curtains and iron. Fold over another 3 cm/1¼ in. Pin, tack and stitch the hems. Fold the tabs in half and pin on to the curtains, leaving 9 cm/3½ in gaps between them. Line up the end of the tabs with the bottom of the hem. Tack and stitch in place. Fold in 1 cm/½ in along the bottom of the curtains and then another 4 cm/1½ in. Pin, tack and stitch the bottom hems.

4 Lay the curtains right side up on a flat surface. Measure lines from the top to the bottom of the curtains, approximately 46 cm/18 in apart. Mark with pins, then draw the lines with a dressmaker's pencil. Mark the positions of the floral motifs approximately 60 cm/24 in apart. Tuck the end of the white cotton string over the top of the curtain. Stitch in place with white thread. Pin the string along the marked line and stitch in place.

5 To sew a floral motif, loop the string to form a petal shape and pin in place. Stitch the petal to the fabric. Repeat until the flower has six petals. Continue stitching the string along the marked pencil line to the bottom of the curtain. When the appliqué is complete, iron the curtains.

MUSLIN CURTAINS

Small details such as curtain clips can be an elegant solution to curtain hanging. The white muslin is a generously long piece, folded in half, allowing a drop 1½ times the length of the window – it really is a simple example of window dressing, but the effect is very stylish. Small brass curtain clips fit over the rail and catch the muslin along the fold.

YOU WILL NEED
dowel, window width
woodstain
spare cloth
drill and drill bit
2 wall plugs and 2 nails
hammer
curtain clips
white muslin
wooden pole

1 Stain a length of dowel by shaking woodstain on to a spare cloth and rubbing the dowel with it. Drill a hole in the wall on either side of the window and insert the wall plugs. Bang in the nails.

2 Clip the muslin along the fold, leaving an equal distance between the clips. Thread the rings on to the dowel and place the dowel over the nails.

3 Spread the rings along the dowel so that the muslin falls in even folds.

4 Knot the front drop of the muslin on to the end of the wooden pole and prop this across the window.

SHELL SHOCKED

Wandering along the seashore collecting shells is a wonderfully therapeutic pastime. After holidaying, rather than simply keeping a selection of shells on the sill, make them into something really special. We have made fine voile curtains and added interest to the heading by making eyelets along the top and threading them with string loops. To complete the light, airy feel make a matching shell-decorated pot.

YOU WILL NEED

iron-on interfacing (if required)

tape measure

dressmaker's scissors

cotton voile, the required drop and 4 x the window width

dressmaker's pins

needle and tacking (basting) thread

iron

sewing machine

matching sewing thread

chrome eyelets

hammer and wooden block

rough natural string

fine beading wire

glue gun

shells

electric drill, with very fine drill bit (optional)

beading needle (optional)

terracotta pot

matt (flat) white emulsion (latex) paint

paintbrush

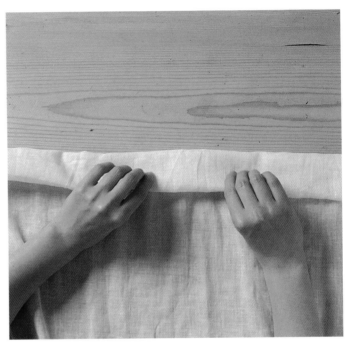

1 To give extra body to the headings of fine fabrics, cut a length of iron-on interfacing 5 cm/2 in wide and bond it to the wrong side of the voile.

2 Pin, tack (baste), press and stitch the heading across the top and the hem at the bottom. Then turn under a 1 cm/½ in hem down each side, pin, tack (baste), press and sew.

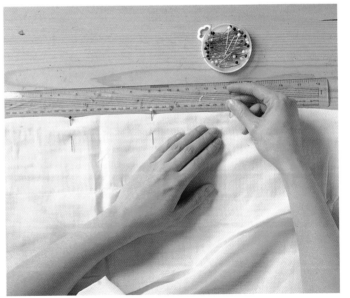

3 Mark the positions of the eyelets with pins at equal distances along the top of the curtain.

4 Fix the eyelets, following the manufacturer's instructions. Make sure you find
a secure surface, such as a wooden
block, when hammering the eyelets in
place. One short, sharp blow with the
hammer should do the trick.

5 Cut equal lengths of string to tie
through the eyelets.

6 Thread the strings through the eyelets
and knot the ends.

7 Cut lengths of fine beading wire and use a glue gun to stick
them on to the shells.

8 Alternatively, drill holes in the shells. You might find a combination of both these methods helpful, depending on the different
shapes of the shells.

9 Position the shells on the curtain, spacing them fairly evenly over the fabric.

10 "Sew" the shells on to the curtain by hand, as invisibly as possible, with the beading wire.

11 Paint the flowerpot with white emulsion (latex) paint.

12 Put a little glue on the side of the pot and attach the shell, holding it in place for a few seconds to ensure that it adheres to the surface.

Above: Even as light filters through the muslin, the wire fixings in the shells remain invisible.

COTTON FRESH

A pair of cotton sheets makes the most wonderful curtain, and all the seams are perfectly finished. The bigger the sheets, the more luxurious the window will look – curtains should always be generous. Wooden pegs can be wedged into a piece of old wooden floorboarding – if you drill the holes at an angle the attachments will be stronger as well as more pleasing to the eye.

YOU WILL NEED
dressmaker's scissors
2.5 m/2½ yd of 2.5 cm/ 1 in wide
cotton tape
2 flat king-size cotton sheets
needle
white sewing thread
drill and drill bit
length of floorboard or driftwood,
window width plus 15 cm/6 in either side
6 old-fashioned wooden pegs
spirit level (carpenter's level)
wallplugs and screws
screwdriver

1 Using sharp scissors, cut the tape into six strips of equal length. These will be used to attach the sheets.

2 Divide the width of each sheet top by three and use the divisions as points to attach the tapes. Fold each tape in half and use small stitches to sew them to the top of the sheet.

3 Drill six holes at equal distances along the floorboard and wedge in the pegs. Drill a hole at either end of the floorboard and screw it into the wall, using a spirit level (carpenter's level) to check it is straight, and appropriate fixings to secure it.

4 Tie the tapes to the wooden pegs and arrange the folds of the fabric to fall evenly across the width of the window.

STRIPED HANGING

This is a wonderfully simple hanging that can be adapted to suit any room or decorative style. Here, striped canvas is hung from a bamboo pole to hide clutter. Alternatively, use calico for a sitting room, muslin for a bedroom, gingham for a kitchen and a cheerful striped deckchair fabric for a child's room. In order to see the hanging clearly, fullness is not required, so the project is extremely economical.

YOU WILL NEED
tape measure
canvas
dressmaker's scissors
dressmaker's pins
needle and tacking (basting) thread
matching sewing thread
dressmaker's pencil
eyelet kit
hammer

1 Measure the width and drop of the area you wish to curtain off and cut the fabric to size, adding 5 cm /2 in extra at the top and bottom. Pin, tack (baste) and sew two lines of stitching.

2 Measure 2.5 cm/1 in from either edge at the top of the curtain and mark the positions. Divide the remaining width of fabric into equal spaces, allowing about 13 cm/5 in between each one.

3 Attach the eyelets at these marked points, following the manufacturer's instructions.

4 On a flat surface, hammer the eyelets firmly into place.

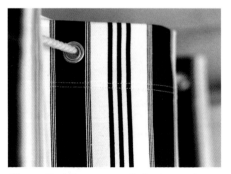

Above: Yachting rope and chrome eyelets complement the fresh blue and white fabric.

CUSHIONED COMFORT

Cushions are the perfect way to add a certain style to your room, as well as an element of comfort. Here, the choice of natural tones and fabrics perfectly complements the simplicity of the sofa. Interest was added to the restrained look with decorative ties, looped buttons and a simple rope trim. If you want more colour, simply add splashes of vibrant blues, reds, oranges and purples.

YOU WILL NEED
about 2 m/2¼ yd fine-gauge rope
plain linen cushion cover
dressmaker's pins
needle
matching sewing threads
dressmaker's scissors
cushion pads
tape measure
cotton duck (canvas)
tacking (basting) thread
sewing machine
iron
1 m/1 yd linen
8–10 small buttons

1 For the rope-trimmed cushion, use the fine-gauge rope to experiment with different designs, then pin the rope on to the cover. Hand stitch the rope to the cover, neatly finishing off the ends. Insert the cushion pad.

2 For the cushion with ties, measure the cushion pad and cut one piece of cotton duck the depth of the cushion plus 1.5 cm/⅝ in all round for seams. Cut another piece to twice the length, plus an extra 16.5 cm/6½ in for the turning (this allows 1.5 cm/⅝ in for a hem also). Pin, tack (baste), press and sew, taking in the seam allowance. Trim and zigzag stitch the raw edges together to neaten them. Turn the cushion right side out.

3 For the ties, cut six pieces of fabric 6 x 28 cm/2¼ x 11 in. Fold each piece in half lengthways with wrong sides together and pin, tack, press and stitch a 1 cm/½ in seam around two sides. Clip the seams and corners. Turn the ties right sides out and slip stitch the ends closed. Position the ties in pairs and pin, tack and topstitch them in position.

4 For the cushion with buttons, measure the width and length of the cushion pad. Double the length and add 10 cm/4 in for the flap opening, plus 3 cm/1¼ in for seams all around. You will also need to cut a 7.5 cm/3 in wide strip, the depth of the cushion plus seams. Cut linen to this size and fold it in half.

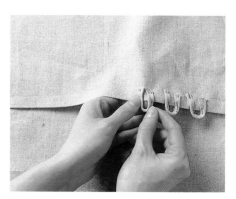

5 Cut a length of fabric 2.5 cm/1 in wide and make up as for the ties in step 3. Measure the buttons and cut the loops to size. Turn over the seam allowance on the cover, then pin the loops in place. Pin and sew the interfacing for the back opening on the edge with the loops. With right sides together, sew round the cushion. Sew the buttons on the right side.

COTTON-DRAPED CHAIR

This effect is stylish and practical and yet needs no sewing skills. To create the right amount of drama, a generous quantity of fabric is essential; this project uses a king-size, pure cotton sheet for each chair, which is ready-hemmed, but you can use any wide, preferably washable, fabric that is soft enough to knot and tie.

YOU WILL NEED
chair
king-size cotton sheet or fabric
sewing machine (optional)
matching sewing thread (optional)

1 You need at least twice, and preferably three times, as much fabric as the width of your chair. Hem the fabric if necessary. Throw the fabric over the chair and centre it.

2 Tuck the fabric down the back behind the seat of the chair. If the chair has arms, do this all around the seat, so that the cover doesn't pull out when you sit on the chair.

3 Sweep the fabric round to the back of the chair.

4 Tie a knot, making sure that the fabric is an even length on both sides and that you have attractive folds and drapes at the sides. Try to tie the knot confidently in one go otherwise the fabric can look tortured and crumpled. Remember that the fabric should cascade down from the knot.

ROMANTIC CHAIR COVER

A beautiful chair might not seem to need further treatment, yet for a change, or for a special occasion, you might want to decorate a chair without masking its integral beauty. A wistful, romantic appeal can be given by swathing the chair in translucent fabric to give it a special softness. Tie the sash that takes up the extra fabric in a knot or a big, soft bow and leave it either at the back or on the seat, like a cushion.

YOU WILL NEED

wooden chair
tissue or pattern-cutting paper
pencil
dressmaker's pins
3 m/3⅜ yd of 137 cm/54 in wide
transparent silk, voile or organza
(organdie)
fabric marker
dressmaker's scissors
tape measure
sewing machine
matching sewing thread
iron

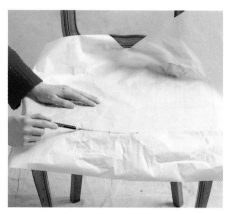

1 Using the paper and pencil, carefully trace the shape of the chair back rest. Use this as a template for cutting out the back and front of the back rest cover, adding 2 cm/¾ in all round for seams. Pin the template to the fabric, draw round it and cut out the pieces.

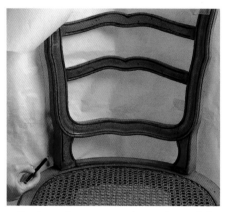

2 Trace the shape of the seat in the same way. Transfer on to the fabric, adding 2 cm/¾ in all round for seam allowances. Measure from the edge of the seat to the floor, for the depth of the skirt, and again add at least 2 cm/¾ in for a seam allowance.

3 For the width of the skirt, add 120 cm/48 in to the circumference of the chair seat, to allow for the corner box pleats. Cut this as one continuous panel. For the sash, allow a 2 m/2¼ yd length of 40 cm/16 in wide fabric.

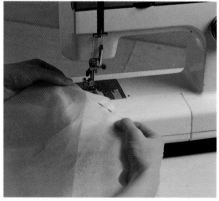

4 Stitch the bottom of the front back rest panel to the top of the seat panel with right sides together. Press open all the seams as you go. With right sides together, stitch the front back rest panel to the back.

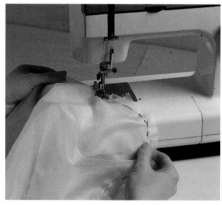

5 Hem the bottom edge of the skirt. Fold, press and pin the pleats, positioning them at the corners. Stitch along the top edge of the skirt panel. Stitch the skirt to the seat panel at the sides and front and to the back panel at the back, positioning the pleats at the corners. Fold the sash in half lengthways, right sides together, and stitch up the long seam and one short seam. Turn the sash right sides out and slip stitch the end. Tie round the chair.

EMBROIDERED PILLOWCASES

Fall asleep to the sound of the seashore with pillowcases that are guaranteed to evoke blue skies, drifts of clouds and foaming waves. The co-ordinating blue and white scheme is gloriously fresh – a chain stitch and a single strand of thread give a delicate feel to the embroidery of the sea creatures and shells adorning the pillowcases.

YOU WILL NEED
pencil
tracing paper
pillowcase
dressmaker's scissors
dressmaker's pins
dressmaker's carbon paper
dressmaker's pencil
needle
soft embroidery thread (floss)
ruler

1 Trace the templates at the back of the book and enlarge if necessary. Cut them out, arrange them around the edge of the pillowcase and pin in place.

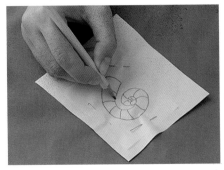

2 Next, pin sheets of dressmaker's carbon paper under the tracing paper in the marked positions. Trace over the images with a dressmaker's pencil to leave a clear outline on the fabric.

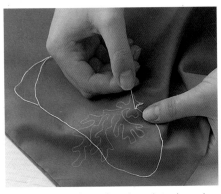

3 Separate the soft embroidery thread (floss) into single strands. Start the chain stitch by making a loop and pushing the needle into the fabric on the outline. Insert the needle through the centre of the loop, following the outline of the motif.

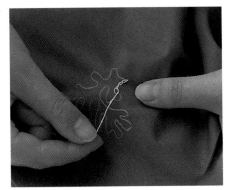

4 Pull the thread taut. Always try to keep stitch lengths and tautness of thread even throughout the embroidery.

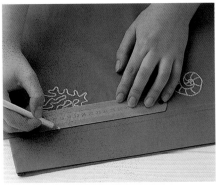

5 Mark an edging with a ruler for the top of the pillowcase.

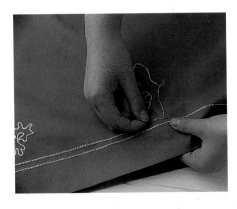

6 Finish the edge of the pillowcase with a simple line of cord or with a double row of chain stitch.

Right: The embroidery and designs are kept deliberately simple.

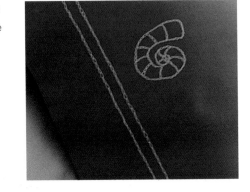

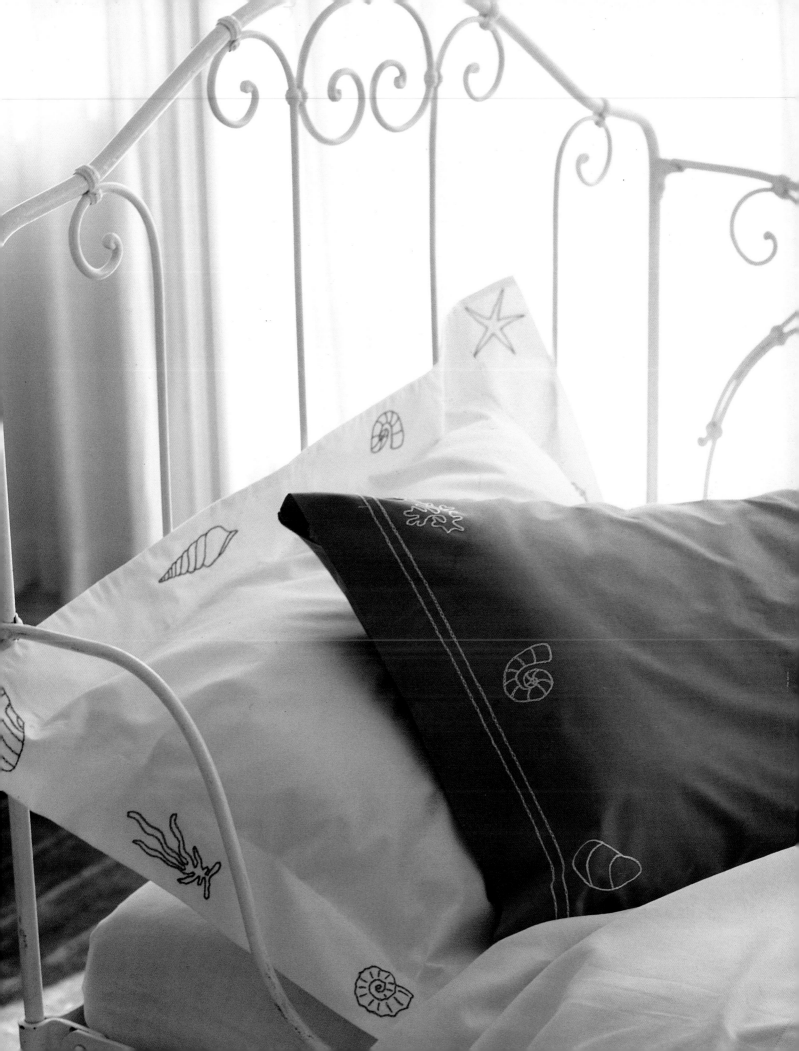

LOVELY LINENS

Pretty up perfectly plain linens with splashes of vibrant colour. To add definition, add ric-rac braid around the edge. For frilliness, buy broderie anglaise and sew this on to the pillowcase, then weave tapestry wool (yarn) through the holes to add colour. Alternatively, look for linens that have a fine-holed edging and thread this with fine tapestry wool.

YOU WILL NEED

paper

pencil

cardboard

scissors

single or double white sheet

sewing machine

white sewing thread

small, pointed scissors

red tapestry wool (yarn)

tapestry needle

plain pillowcase

dressmaker's pins

needle and tacking (basting) thread

3 m/3⅜ yd broderie anglaise (eyelet lace)

buttoned pillowcase, with fine-holed

decorative edge

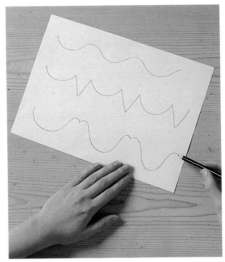

1 Try various designs for the shape of the scalloped edge of the sheet. Transfer your chosen design on to cardboard and cut out the template for the sheet edging.

2 Put the template on the edge of the sheet and draw along the edge. Use machine satin stitch to work over the outline. Very carefully cut out along the sewing line close to the sewing but taking care not to snip any stitches.

3 Cut lengths of tapestry wool (yarn) and knot the ends. Sew the lengths of tapestry wool through the sheet, leaving the long ends to form a decorative edge.

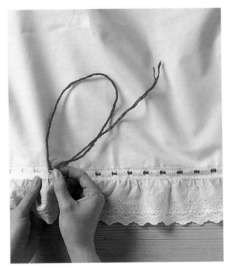

4 Pin and tack (baste) broderie anglaise (eyelet lace) along the edge of the plain pillowcase. Machine stitch in place. Using a tapestry needle, thread the wool through the holes in the broderie anglaise.

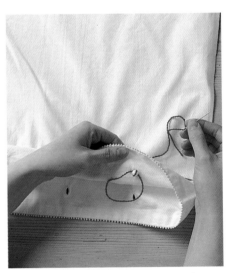

5 For the buttoned pillowcase, make neat cross stitches over the buttons with tapestry wool. Thread tapestry wool through the fine-holed decorative edge.

LACE-TRIMMED BEDLINEN

Nothing looks more romantic than a bed covered with lace-trimmed white bedlinen. Make layers of scallops and frills on sheets, bolsters, pillows and bed covers. Start by buying a good cotton duvet cover with a scalloped edge. Trawl second-hand shops and flea markets for lace-edged tablecloths, dressing table runners, tray cloths and curtains. Look out for old white cotton sheets with embroidered edges, to add interest.

YOU WILL NEED
selection of lacy tablecloths, tray
cloths, mats, chair backs or dressing table
runners
plain white bed linen
dressmaker's pins
iron-on hemming tape or needle and
white sewing thread
iron
bolsters
rubber bands
white ribbon or raffia

1 Select suitably sized pieces of lace to make central panels or corner details on the pillowcases and duvet cover. Pin them in position.

2 Use iron-on hemming tape and an iron to bond the two layers together, or slip stitch them in place.

3 Roll up the bolster in a lace-edged tablecloth and bunch up the ends, securing them with rubber bands.

4 Tie bows of ribbon or raffia over the gathered ends and let the lace edging drape over the edge of the bed.

SHEER MAGIC

Trim a plain linen or hessian (burlap) bed cover and pillowcase with the sheerest of voile fabrics, to give a look which is simple, tailored and very elegant. Large bone buttons and the rougher textures of hessian and linen are the perfect foil to the fineness of the fabric. Cut the voile a tiny bit longer than the drop on the bed so it falls all the way round. The amount of voile fabric given here is for a double bed, but the idea can be adapted to suit any size bed.

YOU WILL NEED

tape measure
about 7 m/7¾ yd cotton voile
dressmaker's scissors
dressmaker's pins
needle and tacking (basting) thread
sewing machine
matching sewing thread
fine embroidery scissors
tapestry needle
16 large bone buttons
fine string
hessian (burlap) or fine linen bed cover
pillow
hessian or fine linen
iron

1 For the top of the cover, you will need a piece of voile the length of the bed plus the drop on one end. The piece should be 15 cm/6 in narrower than the width of the bed so the buttons will not be too near the edge.

2 You will also need to allow 10 cm/4 in all round for double hems. For the sides, you will need two pieces the length of the bed. Measure the drop from the buttons to the floor, allowing extra for hems as before.

3 Pin, tack (baste) and stitch all the hems. Mark the positions of the buttons and buttonholes so they correspond exactly. Sew the buttonholes and cut the centres carefully.

4 Use a tapestry needle to thread fine string through the buttons. Tie the string in a knot. Sew the buttons in position on the hessian (burlap) bed cover, and button the voile cover on top.

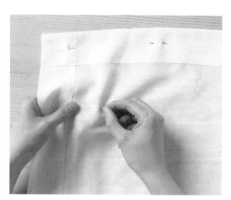

5 For the pillowcase, cut a piece of hessian the depth of the pillow and twice the length, plus seam allowances on the long sides. With right sides together, pin, tack and stitch the top and bottom edges. Turn right side out and press.

6 To make a fringed edge, find a thread running across the pillow, just in from the cut edge. Pull the thread gently to fray the edge.

7 Use the same method to make an over-cover for the pillow from voile. Hem all the edges. Mark the position of the buttonholes in each corner. Machine stitch the buttonholes and cut the centres. Sew buttons on to the corners of the hessian pillow cover, and button the voile cover over the top.

JAPANESE FUTON

This stylish bedroom exudes a typically Japanese sense of order and calm. Wooden pallets were used for the bed base. These come in different sizes, but they can be sawn down and stacked to make a bed of the right size. The beautiful cream cotton bed cover is a decorator's dustsheet (tarp). Such dustsheets are incredibly cheap, so you can have the minimalist look for minimal outlay.

YOU WILL NEED
wooden pallets
medium- and fine-grade sandpaper
light-coloured woodstain
paintbrush
futon mattress
bolster
2 m/2¼ yd black cotton cord
scissors
needle
matching sewing thread
decorator's dustsheet (tarp)
2 black tassels
cream coloured square cushion

1 Prepare the wooden pallets by rubbing them down first with medium-grade, then with fine-grade, sandpaper.

2 Apply a coat of woodstain to seal and colour the wood. Allow to dry thoroughly. Lay the pallets on the floor to make a bed base. Lay the mattress and bolster on the base.

3 Cut six 30 cm/12 in lengths of black cord. Make each length into a loop tied with a reef knot.

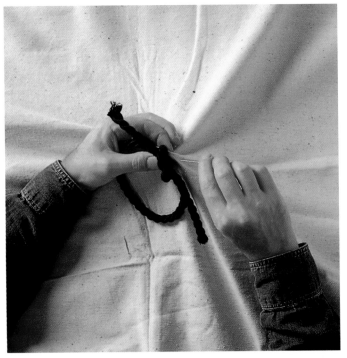

4 Slip stitch the knotted cords on to the dustsheet (tarp) to make three rows of two cords down the centre of the bed. Spread the dustsheet on the bed and fold it over the pillow. Sew two black tassels on to the cushion and place it on the pillows. Tuck the dustsheet under the mattress all the way around the bed.

LEAF ROOM DIVIDER

Created from handmade Japanese washi paper and leaf skeletons from the sacred bodhi tree, this delicate room divider diffuses the daylight, providing a gentle, slightly hazy retreat from bright sunshine. The divider is attached at the top edge only and, because the paper is so light, it will move softly with the slightest breeze. Leaf skeletons can be ordered from specialist suppliers and many florists.

YOU WILL NEED
leaf skeletons
thin Japanese washi paper
dressmaker's pins
sewing machine
matching sewing thread

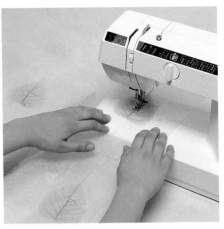

1 Pin rows of leaf skeletons to one side of a sheet of thin Japanese paper. Turn the paper over and pin leaves to the other side, in the same position as the first leaves.

2 Using a long, straight machine stitch, attach the leaves to the paper by stitching along the line of each main vein. Remove the pins from either side of the paper before you reach them.

3 Lay two sheets of paper right sides together and machine stitch along one shorter side to join them. Continue to add more panels in the same way until the divider is the correct length. Make more long strips to fit the desired width.

4 Lay the long strips of paper right sides together so that all the seams are to the back. Machine stitch the long sides to complete the divider.

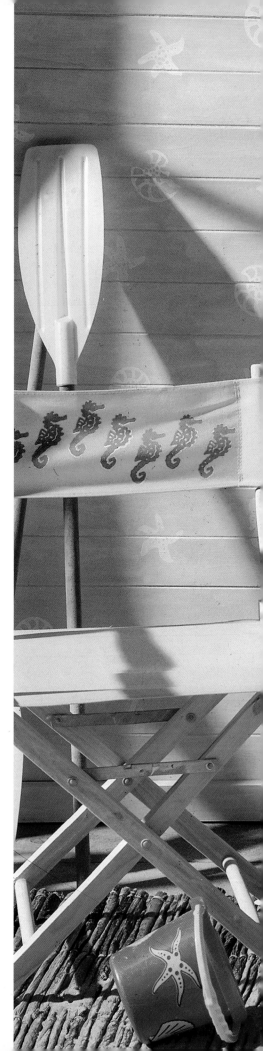

SURFACES

"The wooden walls are the best walls

of this kingdom"

THOMAS COVENTRY

Introduction

"Now stir the fire, and close the shutters fast"
WILLIAM COWPER

Walls and floors are large blank canvases just waiting to be decorated. In small, narrow halls, where there is no room for furniture, the walls and floor are the only source of decoration, so you can be extra inventive. There are many ways to introduce colour and texture to walls, apart from paint and paper: rough plaster, stamps, stencils, tongue-and-groove panelling and tiles can all be used on their own or in combination.

On floors, try out different effects such as varnishing, colour-washing or stamping. Arrange coloured floor tiles in a pattern to create your own mosaic. And for a final touch, add rugs and dhurries for softness.

Above: A chequerboard arrangement of tiles is punctuated by a single, hand-stamped grape motif.

plaster walls

distressed floors

tongue-and-groove panelling

colourwashed shutters

Left: Distressed wood panelling needs no additional embellishment.

Right: Plaster stars decorate a bathroom to dado (chair) rail height.

Below: Plaster walls treated with a distressed rose pattern.

Above left and above: Draw inspiration from the wood found at the seaside to decorate your home.

ROUGH PLASTER WALL

If you are lucky enough to have smooth walls but you want to create a surface texture with a little more interest and depth, you can create a slightly rough plaster wall with this technique, using a little plaster scraped over the surface. Here, a crisp white painted finish evokes whitewashed cottages by the seaside, but the wall could just as well be washed with any colour of your choice.

YOU WILL NEED

plaster filler (spackle)

old bucket

piece of thick cardboard or plywood

white emulsion (latex) paint

paint-mixing container (optional)

paintbrush

1 Following the manufacturer's instructions, mix the plaster filler (spackle) in an old bucket.

2 Wipe it on to the wall with a piece of thick cardboard or plywood so it forms an uneven surface. Leave it to dry.

3 Alternatively, for a slightly smoother result, mix plaster filler and emulsion (latex) paint and brush on.

4 When dry, apply a second coat of paint, rubbing it in well with the paintbrush so all the surfaces are thoroughly covered.

WOODLAND STRIPES

This pretty bedroom is decorated using two very quick, easy and effective techniques. The stripes are applied first on to a white wall, using a small roller. Rolling colour on in this way gives a mottled coverage with slightly wavy edges to give a subtle, faded look. The leaves are stamped diagonally in opposite directions to make a zigzag pattern.

YOU WILL NEED
wallpaper paste
grey, leaf green, deep blue-green, deep red
and dusky pink emulsion (latex) paint
old plates
spirit level (carpenter's level)
5 cm x 2.5 cm/2 in x 1 in wooden
batten (lath)
masking tape
foam (rubber) rollers
medium square-tipped artist's brush
leaf stamp

1 Mix the wallpaper paste, then mix one part wallpaper paste with one part grey emulsion (latex) paint on a large plate. The mixture will produce a slightly translucent glaze when dry. Tape the spirit level (carpenter's level) to the wooden batten with masking tape.

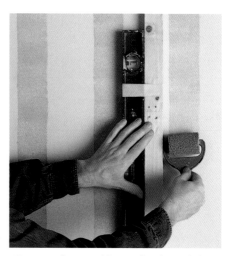

2 Run a foam (rubber) roller through the paint until it is evenly coated. Hold the batten-ruler in one corner of the wall and run the roller down its edge to the dado (chair) rail or skirting board (baseboard). Line up the ruler with the edge of the stripe and continue rolling across the wall.

3 Using a paintbrush and grey paint, complete the stripes at the ceiling and dado rail or skirting board, where the roller has not reached.

4 Mix one part leaf green emulsion paint with one part wallpaper paste on a plate and use to ink the leaf stamp. Stamp columns of leaves between the grey stripes. Stamp the leaves diagonally, changing the direction of the stamp to create a zigzag pattern.

5 Continue stamping until all the white stripes are filled. Re-ink the stamp when the print becomes very pale, but do allow some variety in the depth of colour of the prints. This irregularity will emphasize the feel of hand-blocked wallpaper.

TUSCAN DOORWAY

With patience and a little confidence, you can attempt a simple trompe l'oeil wall decoration, to create the feel of a Tuscan country house in your own home. The key to achieving this rustic look is to layer the colours and then rub the layers back to reveal some of the colours underneath, as though there has been a build-up of paint over the years. A final wash of watery ochre enhances the aged look.

YOU WILL NEED
cream, warm yellow, terracotta and green
emulsion (latex) paint
paintbrushes in different sizes
scrap paper
paint roller
paint-mixing tray
pencil
set square (T square) or ruler
spirit level (carpenter's level)
straight edge
string
masking tape
hand sander
brown pencil

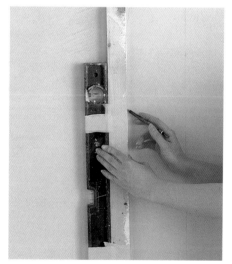

1 Experiment with colours. You can pick quite strong shades as they will soften when they are sanded.

2 Apply the cream base coat with a paint roller. Wash over this with a warm yellow using a large paintbrush.

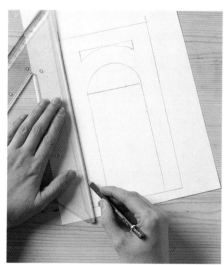

3 Draw your design to scale on paper using a set square (T square) or ruler.

4 Measure and draw the straight lines on the wall, using the spirit level (carpenter's level) and straight edge.

5 Draw the curve, using a pencil tied to a length of string.

▶

6 Mask off the areas of terracotta colour with masking tape.

7 Paint in the terracotta areas and immediately remove the tape.

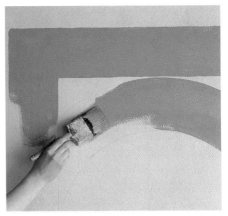

8 Paint the other areas green, masking off other areas if necessary.

9 Paint a thin yellow outline around all the edges by hand.

10 Lightly sand over the design, going back to the base coat in some areas and leaving others untouched. Wash over everything again with the warm yellow.

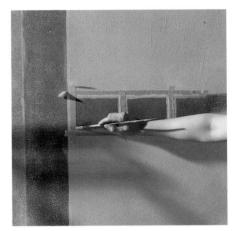

11 Mask off the squares in the border. Paint the outlines and immediately remove the tape.

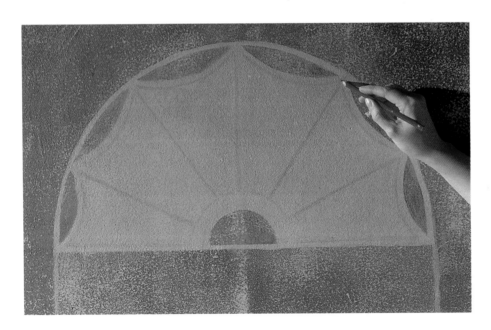

12 Use the brown pencil to draw in extra fine lines in the semi-circular "fanlight" ("transom").

STAMPED WALL PANELS

Bring large areas of decoration to a wall with these easy panels. Painting or dragging panels over a base coat quickly gives interest to large expanses of wall. It's a good idea to connect the panel and wall area outside visually with a simple motif. This could be a strong modern shape, wavy lines or even flowers. The colour of the walls and the style of motif give scope for a wide range of different looks.

YOU WILL NEED

cream, white and black emulsion
(latex) paint
paint roller
paint-mixing tray
spirit level (carpenter's level)
straight edge
pencil
masking tape
dragging brush
scrap paper
scissors
high-density foam (rubber)
glue
craft knife
tape measure
old plate
small foam (rubber) roller

1 To prepare the wall for stamping, apply a base coat of cream emulsion (latex) paint.

2 Using the spirit level (carpenter's level) and straight edge, draw the outlines for the panels on the wall.

3 Mask off the outer edge of the panels with masking tape.

4 Drag white emulsion paint over the base coat.

5 Design the stamp motif on paper. Use cut-out shapes stuck to the wall to plan your finished design. The motifs used here are clean and contemporary-looking, but more traditional or figurative designs can also be used. ▶

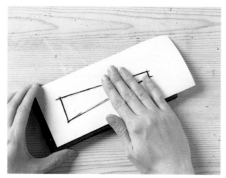

6 Stick your chosen motif to the high-density foam (rubber).

7 With the craft knife, cut out the unwanted areas of the design to leave a raised stamp. Angle the cut outwards slightly from the top to bottom of the foam to give a cleaner finish to the stamped motifs.

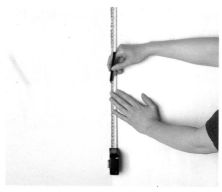

8 Decide on the spacing of the stamps and mark the positions on the wall.

9 Put some black paint on to the plate, run the small roller through it until it is evenly coated and then roll the paint on to the stamp.

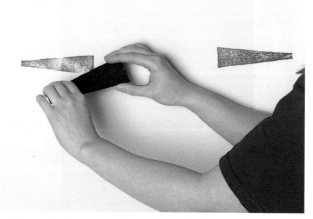

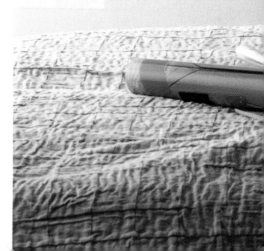

10 Stamp the design in the marked positions. For a textured effect, make more than one print without reloading the stamp.

PAPER PANELS

Sometimes the simplest ideas are the most effective. Brown paper has its own characteristic colour and texture that look wonderful on walls. You can buy the paper on rolls, which makes papering under a dado rail (chair rail) simplicity itself. Here the paper has been combined with gum arabic tape (rubber cement tape) for an unusual and elegant design.

YOU WILL NEED
brown paper
wallpaper paste
pasting brush
plumb line
straight edge
pencil
gum arabic tape (rubber cement tape)
paintbrush
spirit level (carpenter's level)
black beading
glue gun and glue sticks

1 Stick the brown paper to the wall with the matt side inwards, using wallpaper paste and a pasting brush. Smooth out any air bubbles.

2 Use a plumb line and straight edge to mark guides for the stripes. Using a paintbrush, wet the wall in strips the width of the tape, and stick down.

3 Use a spirit level (carpenter's level) and straight edge to draw a horizontal guide line for the top border. Stick the tape in place as before.

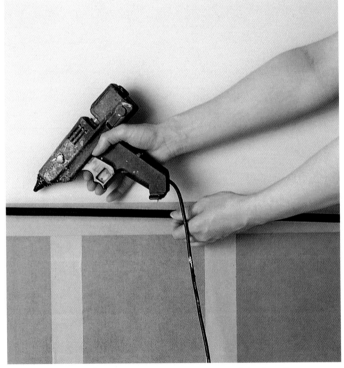

4 Attach the black beading along the top of the border, using the glue gun and glue sticks. Hold the beading in place for a few seconds until the glue has set, then continue around the wall.

ROPE DECORATION

A pattern in rope makes a simple, textured wall finish, perfectly in keeping with today's trend for natural materials in interiors. As rope makes good curves, the design can twist and turn as much as you like. For a small area or to make a focal point in a room, mark out squares and put a different, simple design in each square. You could also use the rope to create borders at dado rail (chair rail) and picture rail height.

YOU WILL NEED
scrap paper
pencil
spirit level (carpenter's level)
straight edge
rope
glue gun or strong adhesive
empty paint cans (optional)
masking tape
craft knife
white emulsion (latex) paint
paintbrush

1 Plan and draw your design to scale on paper.

2 Transfer to the wall using a spirit level (carpenter's level) and straight edge.

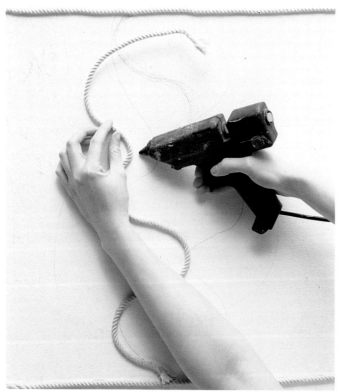

3 Use a glue gun or other suitable adhesive to attach the rope to the wall. Use paint cans or other round objects to help you to make smooth curves. It is easier to cut the rope if you wrap masking tape around it, and cut through the tape.

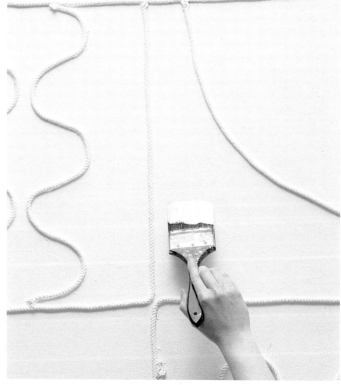

4 Paint over the wall and rope with white emulsion (latex) paint; you may need a few coats to get an even finish.

CRACKLE GLAZE SHUTTERS

Crackle glaze is an excellent medium for ageing new doors, shutters or even furniture. It is easy to apply, and when sealed with a matt (flat) varnish it provides a permanent finish. The crackle glaze should be applied between two layers of water-based emulsion (latex) paint. This sandwich of paint/glaze/paint allows the surface of the glaze to crack and split, creating a peeled patina reminiscent of ageing paint.

YOU WILL NEED
wooden shutters
old cloths
medium-grade sandpaper
aqua and blue emulsion (latex) paint
paintbrush
crackle glaze

1 Dust and clean the wood on shutters to prepare them for treatment.

2 Rub down the surface of the shutter with sandpaper to provide a key, then buff it up with a soft cloth.

3 Apply two coats of aqua paint to the shutter, letting it dry thoroughly between coats.

4 Apply a thin coat of crackle glaze all over the surface of the shutter and let it dry thoroughly.

5 Water down some blue paint, 2 parts water to 1 part paint, and apply it to the surface. Leave it to dry and crack.

6 Gently sand over the blue paint to distress and to let the crackle glaze and aqua paint show through.

WASHED FLOORBOARDS

Liming floorboards creates a soft, weathered look that is reminiscent of a Scandinavian interior. This effect can also be achieved by simply bleaching the boards and scrubbing them – this leaves the boards looking fresh, but you must be prepared to scrub them on a regular basis to avoid any staining and darkening. Sand the floorboards before beginning work on this project.

YOU WILL NEED
wire brush
small tube of white zinc pigment or tint
raw linseed oil
mixing bowl
old spoon
old cloth
matt (flat) varnish
wide paintbrush

1 To prepare the floorboards, stroke the boards with a wire brush, working gently in the direction of the grain. Mix the tube of zinc into the linseed oil. About 2 litres/3½ pints of the mixture covers 21 sq m/25 sq yd.

2 Apply the zinc mixture to the floor-boards with a cloth, rubbing against the grain to start with.

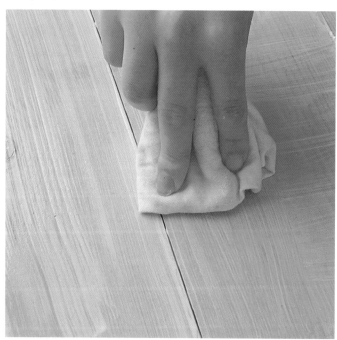

3 Work the mixture into the floorboards, rubbing with the grain. Leave it to dry thoroughly.

4 Seal with a clear matt (flat) varnish, or just apply another layer of white zinc when the first treatment wears away.

PEBBLE DASH PAVING

Pebbles, cobbles and stone have all been used the world over to create beautifully classic yet hardwearing floors. Many floors, such as those found on the Greek islands, are fashioned into incredible mosaic designs. Others depict nautical subjects such as an anchor or a ship and compass. The simple chequerboard design here looks stunning in its simplicity and is, in fact, not at all difficult to create.

YOU WILL NEED
sharp sand
cement
straight edge
tiles
hammer
pebbles
soft brush
watering can, with a fine spray nozzle

1 Mix equal quantities of sharp sand and cement. Pour this dry mortar on to the flat surface to be paved. Using a straight edge, level it out until it is smooth. Remove a small quantity so that the mixture does not overflow as you work.

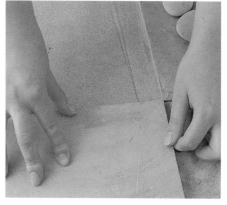

2 Position the tiles, creating alternate squares in a chequerboard effect, making sure they are absolutely square. Hammer them firmly into position and check that once the pebbles are inserted the floor will be level.

3 Arrange your pebbles in a pleasing design, then press them firmly into place. If necessary, hammer them in.

4 Brush dry mortar evenly over the finished surface. Using a watering can, dampen the surface. As the mortar absorbs the moisture, it will set hard.

SLATTED DECKING

Decking immediately brings to mind boats and marinas, with the sound of splashing water in the background. This slatted bath mat is made from strips of wood and can be used either in the shower or as a mat on which to step out of the bath. Use a hardwood to withstand water, and make sure that it is treated with a water-resistant matt (flat) yacht varnish when finished to help preserve it.

YOU WILL NEED
hardwood slats, 5 cm x 2.5 cm/2 in x 1 in
saw
medium-grade sandpaper
ruler
pencil
bradawl
wood glue
brass screws
screwdriver
matt (flat) yacht varnish
paintbrush

1 Decide on the size of your bath mat. Allowing for 2.5 cm/1 in between slats, calculate how many slats you need. Cut the wood to size. Sand the ends of the pieces.

2 Cut two lengths of wood to act as the cross-pieces on to which all the slats are attached. Mark them at regular intervals where the slats will be.

3 Using a bradawl, make holes for the brass screws at the marked points.

4 Mark on the back of each end of the wood slats where the cross-pieces will go. Place a small amount of wood glue on these marks.

5 Position the cross-pieces on top of the slats, matching up all the marks. Secure them in place with brass screws. Finish the mat with a coat of yacht varnish.

CORK-STAMPED FLOORBOARDS

This aesthetically pleasing stamp has been made from seven wine bottle corks. They have been taped together in a daisy-shaped bundle, and the pattern shapes have been cut from the surface of the cork bundle with a craft knife. Dense cork like this is a wonderful material to carve into, being both soft and very smooth. We have used it as a border, but it could also be spaced across the floor as an all-over pattern.

YOU WILL NEED
7 wine bottle corks
scrap paper
wood glue or PVA (white) glue
strong tape
tracing paper
pencil
felt-tipped pen
craft knife
2 paper strips of equal width
dark woodstain
bowl
kitchen paper (paper towels)

1 Stand the corks in a daisy formation on a sheet of paper. Apply a line of glue to all their meeting edges. Make sure that all their ends are flat. When the glue has become tacky, tightly bind with strong adhesive tape.

2 Trace the template below and enlarge if necessary. Copy the pattern shape with a felt-tipped pen on to the flat surface of the corks.

3 Cut away all the background pieces with a craft knife. The pattern can be made more complex by cutting grooves in the smooth cork surface. Before printing, ensure the floor surface is totally dust-free.

4 Lay the two paper strips against the skirting board (baseboard) in both directions from a corner as guides. Stand the stamp in a bowl of woodstain for 10 minutes, then blot on kitchen paper (paper towels). Make the first stamp in the corner.

5 Move the spacing strips into the next corner and stamp the second print.

6 Move the strips along the straight skirting board section and stamp a motif about halfway between the first two. Stamp a row of evenly spaced motifs between the existing prints. Continue to stamp a border around the room.

FURNITURE

"And might proud I am ... that I am able to have

a spare bed for friends"

SAMUEL PEPYS

Introduction

"...and who shall dare
To chide me for loving that old arm-chair"
ELIZA COOK

Whether you are making new furniture or renovating old pieces, wood is the natural starting point. Old wood has great character, and it needn't be expensive. Packing cases and pallets are readily available and are ideal for dismantling before cutting to size and sanding smooth. Accessories such as string, shells and twigs add the finishing touches or can be used to completely cover items, such as a string-covered chair. Finally, a coat of paint or stamped designs give your wooden furniture the designer look. For an equally natural look, make a canvas canopy to give your bed style.

Above: A design classic is given a contemporary lift with bright, bold stripes.

Above and left: Reclaimed pallets make a simple bedhead. A charmingly distressed bedside table is the perfect complement.

driftwood shelves

trellis headboards

canvas canopies

rope-wrapped chairs

Above: A hard-wearing cabinet made from reclaimed boards.

Above: The simple beauty of fittings from the past is incontestable.

Far left: A junk shop find embellished with decoupage motifs.

Left: Strong shapes in pleasing materials are unbeatable.

ROPE-WRAPPED CHAIR

Wrapped in sisal rope, a battered old junk shop chair not only acquires a new lease of life as a beautiful piece of furniture but becomes an object of almost sculptural impact. It doesn't matter how damaged the surface of the chair is, as it will be completely covered by the rope, but try to find one that has a pleasing basic shape. Old-fashioned wooden kitchen chairs would be very suitable.

YOU WILL NEED
nicely shaped wooden chair
medium-grade sandpaper
wood filler
sisal rope
extra-strong white glue
glue spreader
craft knife
cutting mat
large clips

1 Prepare the chair by cleaning and sanding it to remove any paint or varnish that will prevent the glue from adhering. Repair any major damage with wood filler to provide a smooth, even surface. Leave it to dry thoroughly, then sand off any excess.

2 Wrap the rope around the back rail of the chair, gluing it securely in place. Glue lengths of rope across the back of the seat of the chair and cut them off at the back uprights using a craft knife and cutting mat. Glue lengths of rope across the front of the seat, following the curve carefully. Cut short lengths of rope to glue on to the back uprights next to the back rail.

3 Cut a few short lengths of rope, each one slightly shorter than the next. Glue the short lengths of rope in place to form a triangle on the upright at each side of the back rail (see step 7).

4 Wrap the brace between the legs of the chair, adding triangles of rope at the intersections, as before. Begin to wrap the arm rail of the chair, working from the seat upwards. Use large clips to hold the rope in place while the glue dries.

5 Add more rope across the front of the seat until the edges are aligned with the rope wrapping the arm rail.

▶

6 Holding the rope securely in place with the clips while the glue dries, carefully cut off the excess rope.

7 Glue another length of rope across the back of the seat, just in front of the uprights.

8 Wrap the legs, making sure that all the intersections have a triangle of short lengths of rope, as before.

9 Wrap and glue rope around the top rail of the chair. Bring the rope down the arm rail and glue in place. Make sure the rope is exactly in line with the arm of the chair.

10 Wrap and glue an additional length of rope around the front of each arm to conceal any raw edges.

11 Holding the end securely in a clip, glue rope diagonally over the seam between the top rail and each back upright. Similarly, overwrap any other seams that need to be either concealed or embellished.

12 Glue a length of rope across the centre of the seat from the back to the front, holding the end with a clip. Trim to length. Add more lengths of rope on either side of this first length to cover the seat completely.

Right: The rope emphasizes the original lines of the chair while adding a new tactile quality.

GILDED CHAIR

Many a beautiful antique bentwood chair is relegated to the attic because its cane seat has become worn or damaged. Re-caning is expensive and it is hard to find skilled craftsmen to do it, but with some effort and very little extra expense you can set in a solid seat. With a dramatic gold leaf decoration, the chair can become the star of the room. A good art shop can supply the correct size, gold leaf and varnish.

YOU WILL NEED
wooden chair
craft knife
small screwdriver or bradawl
4 wooden blocks
pencil
saw
drill with wood bit
8 wood screws
screwdriver
sheet of paper
scissors
sheet of plywood
masking tape
jigsaw (optional)
medium-grade sandpaper
paintbrush
gold size
Dutch gold leaf
clean, dry paintbrush
clean, dry cloth
varnish

1 If the seat needs repairing, cut away the cane with a sharp craft knife.

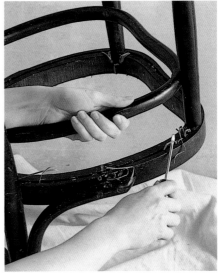

2 Using a screwdriver or bradawl, pick out the remaining strands of cane. To make the corner blocks that will support the new seat, hold the pieces of wood inside each corner, mark the shape of the corners on the wood and then cut the pieces to shape.

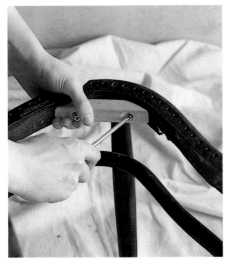

3 Hold a corner block in position and drill through it into the chair. Screw the block into position with wood screws. Repeat for all four corners.

4 Lay the paper over the seat and trace around the shape. Cut out around the shape to create the template.

5 Tape the template to the plywood and draw around it. Cut around the line. A timber merchant (lumber yard) can do this for you if you do not have a jigsaw. ▶

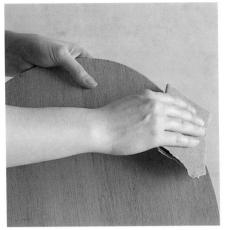

6 Sand the edges of the wooden seat to fit and drop it into place.

7 Prepare the chair for gilding by sanding all the surfaces lightly. Roughening the wood helps the size to adhere.

8 Paint the chair with size and allow it to dry. Follow the manufacturer's recommendations.

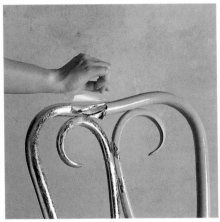

9 Holding the gold leaf by the backing paper, lay a sheet on the chair.

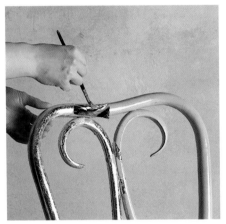

10 With a clean, dry brush, rub the gold leaf on to the chair. Continue until the chair is covered. It is very important that both the brush and your hands are clean and dry.

11 Gently and evenly rub the chair with a clean, dry cloth, to remove any loose flakes.

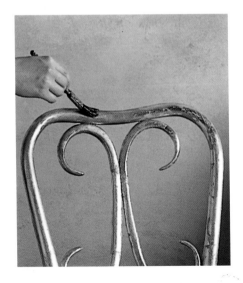

12 Finally, to protect the gold leaf from wear, seal the whole chair with several coats of varnish, leaving to dry between coats.

Right: This treatment could be used on any chair that has graceful lines and surface areas that are not too large. If you want to treat a chair with a wooden back and seat in this way, add more charm by drilling patterns such as heart shapes.

BUCKET STOOL

Florist's buckets in galvanized tin are widely available in a variety of heights; obviously, the taller they are, the better. Cover the seat pad in any fabric (a waffle towel was used here). For a bathroom you could fill a vinyl or a clear plastic seat pad with foam chips in seaside colours or fun sponges in fish or animal shapes. Tea (dish) towels also make striking covers and a layer of dried lavender would make a lovely scented seat.

YOU WILL NEED

1 m/1 yd heavy cord or rope

2 florist's buckets

glue gun

3 very large self-cover buttons

scraps of material for covering buttons

fabric-cutting tool for buttons

waffle hand towel

circular cushion pad

large sewing needle

matching sewing thread

1 Attach the length of cord or rope to the top rim of one of the buckets with the glue gun.

2 Place this bucket inside the second bucket, applying glue to its rim, then invert both buckets.

3 Use the fabric to cover the buttons following the manufacturer's instructions. The special tool used for cutting the fabric is invaluable for this job.

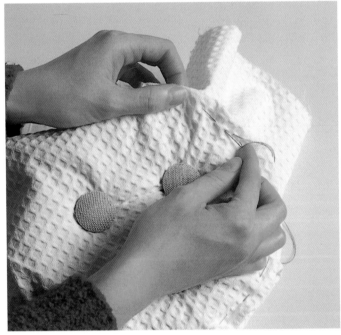

4 Sew the buttons to the centre of the waffle hand towel. Then use the towel to cover the cushion pad. Instead of smoothing out the gathering in the fabric, accentuate it using the buttons as a focus. To finish, glue the pad to the upturned bucket.

ROPE-TRIMMED SOFA

Trim a perfectly plain sofa with a strand of rope that curves gently down the edge of the arm and across the base. This works extremely well in a white-on-white scheme because the eye is aware of the shape but the embellishment doesn't jump out. Other types of trimming for sofas could be raffia edging, linen tassels or fringing.

YOU WILL NEED
graph or plain paper
pencil
rope, the length of the area you wish to trim
clear sticky tape
scissors
dressmaker's pins
needle
strong matching sewing thread

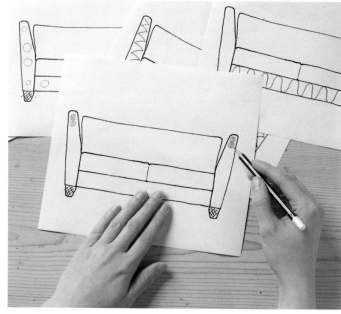

1 Work out different designs for the rope on paper, to see what works the best; this style seemed sympathetic to the shape of the arm of the sofa and the lines of the seat.

2 Bind clear sticky tape around the ends of the rope, so that the ends don't fray once the rope is in position.

3 Cut as close to the end of the tape as you can, so that a little tape is left but it still holds the rope firmly. Pin the rope on to the sofa and hand stitch in place.

SCALLOP-HINGED CUPBOARD

This weathered-looking bathroom cupboard is made from planks of driftwood and wittily uses two pairs of scallop shells as its hinges. The window in the door can be screened from behind with an old string fishing net. To mount the cupboard on the wall, drill holes through the back and screw through them from the inside of the cupboard into matching plugged holes drilled into the wall.

YOU WILL NEED
ruler
pencil
saw
planks of driftwood or
weathered wood
hammer
corrugated fixers (heavy-duty staples)
5 cm/2 in nails
wooden battens
file
2 concave scallop shells
2 flat scallop shells
two brass hinges
reusable tacky putty
drill
8 x 6 mm/¼ in bolts
nuts
screwdriver
12 x 4 cm/1½ in brass screws

1 Measure and saw the planks into nine 50 cm/20 in lengths, six 19.5 cm/7½ in lengths and two 22 cm/8½ in lengths.

2 Join three 50 cm/20 in planks for the back and two pairs of 50 cm/20 in planks for the sides by hammering in a corrugated fixer (staple) at the top and bottom of each join. To make the top, bottom and shelf, join together three pairs of 19.5 cm/7½ in planks in the same way.

3 Turn each section over and hammer in another corrugated fixer at the centre of each join.

4 To make the door, arrange two 22 cm/8½ in planks between two 50 cm/20 in planks, as shown. Nail a batten across the planks at the bottom and top of the door. Turn the door over and hammer in a corrugated fixer at the top and bottom of each join.

5 Position the back on top of the sides and nail together from the back.

6 Insert the top and bottom panels and nail them to the side panels from the outside. Attach the shelf in the same way.

7 File the edges of all the scallop shells to smooth them.

8 File across the joining edge of each shell so that the hinge will lie flush against the shell.

9 Place a hinge over the joining edge of each shell. Hold in place using the reusable tacky putty and mark the positions of the holes.

10 Drill through the marked points on each shell, then drill three evenly spaced holes around the curved edge of each scallop shell.

11 Bolt the hinges on to the shells, pairing each concave shell with a flat one. Fix with nuts on the outside.

12 Drill holes around the edge of the cupboard where you want to attach the hinges. Screw the flat half of each pair of shells on to the side of the cupboard through the holes.

13 Screw the concave half of each shell on to the door in the same way.

PACKING CRATE SHELVES

These charmingly rustic shelves are created from a cast-off pallet, but you could use an orange box. The charm of these shelves is that they have a rather naive quality, so there is no need to worry if the edges are a bit rough or uneven – that is all part of the effect. To finish off the shelves, wash them with diluted paint: try strong Mediterranean colours for a sunny impact or a soft grey-blue reminiscent of the sea.

YOU WILL NEED

wooden pallet or orange box
hammer
pliers
ruler
pencil
saw
strong wood glue
nails
sandpaper
length of square-edged dowel
drill (optional)
string (optional)

1 Dismantle the pallet or orange box with the hammer and pliers. Decide the size shelves you want. Measure and cut the shelf and back to the same length. Saw two pieces for the end sections.

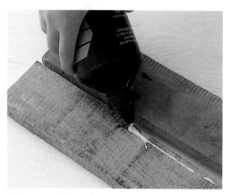

2 Run a line of strong wood glue down the back edge of the base of the shelf. Press the two pieces of wood firmly together to create a right angle. Leave it to dry thoroughly.

3 Insert the end pieces into the right angles at either end of the shelf, and hammer three nails in each side to hold firmly in place.

4 Sand the wood down to create a smooth surface as a key for the paint.

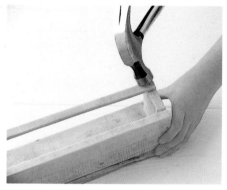

5 Take a length of dowel and secure it in position with nails to form a rail across the front of the shelf.

6 For another style of shelf, drill a hole through each end piece and thread a piece of string through, knotting the string at each end to secure.

Right: The unfinished quality of the shelf is enhanced by seaside finds.

HANGING SHELVES

Create a stunning hanging shelf unit using a single floorboard. Woodstain and a wash of emulsion (latex) paint give the surface a distressed finish. Knotted rope is the perfect partner to blend with the distressed wood and give a real nautical air. If you are looking for something more eye-catching, just paint or stain the shelves in a brighter colour or use warm blues or grey-greens to create a cool look.

YOU WILL NEED

floorboard or plank of wood

saw

pencil

ruler

drill

medium-grade sandpaper

woodstain

old cloths

white emulsion (latex) paint

paintbrush

paint-mixing container

matt (flat) varnish (optional)

4 lengths of rope

masking tape

glue gun

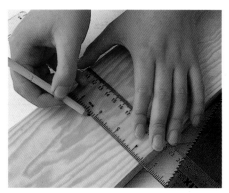

1 Saw the floorboard or wood plank into three pieces of equal length, depending on how long you want your shelves to be. Each piece should be 2.5 cm/1 in wider than the next. Using a pencil and ruler, measure and mark two holes at each end of the three shelf pieces. They should all align where you want the rope to go through. Drill holes through the marks you have made on each of the three pieces of wood. Rub down the wood with sandpaper to make sure it is smooth.

2 Wipe the stain evenly over the pieces of shelving using a clean cloth. Leave it to dry. Dilute the white paint, four parts paint to one part water, and apply a thin wash to the shelves. Using a soft, absorbent cloth, rub away most of the white paint to leave a distressed look. Coat the wood with matt (flat) varnish, if desired, to prevent staining once in use.

3 Take two lengths of rope and wind masking tape around the ends. Knot one end of each rope and thread the other ends through the two holes on one end of the widest shelf. Mark two positions on the rope at the desired height on the middle shelf and tie a knot.

4 Thread the rope through the middle shelf. Mark two positions with masking tape at the height you want the top shelf to hang. Tie a secure knot.

5 Thread the rope through the top shelf. Using a glue gun, glue all the knots to the holes to secure the shelves. Knot the rope firmly at the top of the third shelf as shown, and glue it firmly in place.

STAMPED SHELF

The simple heart shape has been used in folk art around the world for centuries. Here, the heart shape was drawn in four positions on a high-density foam (rubber) block, then cut out to make a stamp that resembles a four-leafed clover. The smaller heart fits neatly along the edges of the shelf supports.

YOU WILL NEED
country-style shelf
two shades of background colour, and deep red acrylic or emulsion (latex) paint
paintbrush
soft cloth
medium-grade sandpaper
tracing paper
pencil
craft knife
spray adhesive
high-density foam (rubber)
old plate

1 Paint the shelf with one coat of the background colour, then rub it back slightly with a damp cloth. Leave it to dry. Apply a second coat of paint and rub it back in the same way. When dry, apply a final lighter coat of paint on top. Leave to dry, then sand down to reveal some of the grain and layers of colour. Trace the template at the back of the book and enlarge if necessary. Cut out the shapes, lightly spray them with adhesive and place on the foam (rubber). Cut around the outline of the shapes with a craft knife.

2 Cut out the single heart shape. First cut the outline, then part the foam (rubber) and cut all the way through. Use the stamp as a measuring guide to estimate the number of prints that will fit comfortably along the back of the shelf. Mark their positions lightly in pencil. Spread an even coating of deep red paint on an old plate.

3 Make a test print of the clover leaf stamp on scrap paper to ensure that the stamp is not overloaded with paint. (You may find it easier to apply paint to the stamp with a paintbrush.) Following the pencil guidelines, press the stamp into the paint and make the first print on the wood.

4 Continue until you have completed all the clover-leaf shapes. Try not to get the finish too even and mechanical; this is a rustic piece of furniture and an uneven finish will be more suitable.

5 Finish off the shelf with a row of small hearts along the support edges, then add small ones between each of the larger motifs.

TWIG HEADBOARD

Dress up the wall behind a bed with an unusual trellis made from woven twigs and branches. The trellis is very lightweight and is easily fixed in place. Continue the theme with twig accessories, crisply starched white sheets and pretty cushion covers. Country garden centres are always worth a visit, because trelliswork like this is handmade and producers often use local garden centres as outlets.

YOU WILL NEED
garden raffia
scissors
handmade twig trellis
masonry nails or cavity wall fixtures
hammer

1 Divide the raffia into two bunches of about twelve strands each. Knot one end of each bunch.

2 Plait the strands to make two braids about 10 cm/4 in long.

3 Tie on to the trellis about 25 cm/ 10 in from each end.

4 Use masonry nails or cavity wall fixtures to attach the plaits to the wall above the bed, suspending the trellis behind the bed.

WOODEN HEADBOARD

Here, a wooden pallet has been rescued and transformed into a headboard for a bed. It could also be used to create a cupboard or tabletop. With a quick coat of paint, the crude wood becomes an object that would be equally at home in a modern apartment or a country cottage. The pallet retains its natural roughness due to the different widths of the planks and nail holes – but the end result is one of charm and simplicity.

YOU WILL NEED
wooden pallet or orange box
hammer
pliers
ruler
pencil
saw
nails
coarse-grade sandpaper
white emulsion (latex) paint
paintbrush
paint-mixing container
matt (flat) varnish (optional)

1 Remove the nails and struts of wood from the pallet or orange box using a hammer and pliers.

2 Decide on the height and width of the headboard. Measure and cut the wood to size, ensuring you have enough pieces for the desired width.

3 Make the back of the headboard by nailing four pieces of wood together, plus a piece attached centrally for stability.

4 Nail the varying widths of wood to this frame to form the front of the headboard. Sand down all the wood to prevent splinters from forming.

5 Paint the headboard with two coats of watered-down white emulsion (latex) paint so the grain shows through. If desired, finish the headboard with a coat of matt (flat) varnish.

CALICO CANOPY

This canopy could make a novelty bedhead for a child's bedroom or a stylish feature in an adult's contemporary bedroom. The canopy is made using a combination of fittings intended for different purposes. The chrome rods are shower rails, finished off in copper with plumber's pipe caps. The fabric used here is unbleached calico, but you could use striped cotton duck or canvas if you prefer.

YOU WILL NEED

8 m/8¾ yd of 90 cm/36 in wide calico

tape measure

pencil

ruler

dressmaker's scissors

6 m/6½ yd iron-on hemming tape

iron

hacksaw

150 cm/60 in length of chrome shower rail

centre punch

hammer

drill, with bit (the size of the copper tube)

1 m/1 yd narrow copper tube

long-nosed pliers

3 chrome shower rail sockets

spirit level (carpenter's level)

screwdriver

6 chrome cup hooks and wallplugs

4 m/4⅜ yd white cord

3 copper pipe caps (to fit shower rail)

1 Decide upon the height of the top of the canopy. Measure off the fabric and tear it to size. Tear in the direction of the weave for a straight line.

2 Fold the calico fabric in four to find the centre, and mark this point.

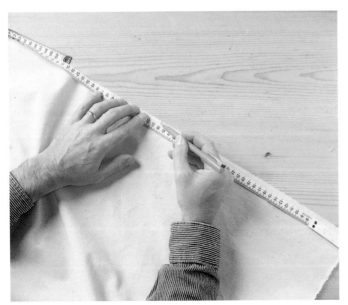

3 Measure 36 cm/14½ in down each short edge and mark the points with a pencil.

4 Lightly draw a connecting line between the centre point and each of the side points. This will create the shape for the top of the canopy.

5 Cut along the drawn lines, then cut a 3 cm/1¼ in notch at each of the points of the canopy shape. Fold the fabric over to make a 3 cm/1¼ in seam around the top and sides of the fabric.

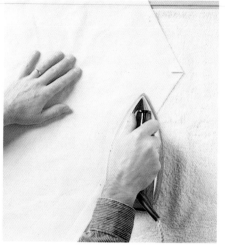

6 Use iron-on hemming tape to hold down the seams neatly. The two pieces should now meet at a right angle to make the canopy shape. The sides and top of the canopy will fold back to give a double thickness of fabric. Make three holes for the rails at the corner points and reinforce the fabric with an extra square of calico ironed on with hemming tape.

7 Use a hacksaw to cut the length of chrome shower rail into three 50 cm/20 in pieces.

8 Use a centre punch to dent the shower rail where the holes will be drilled, so that the drill does not slip. You will need to drill a hole 5 cm/2 in from one end of two of the poles, and two holes in the other pole, the first 5 cm/2 in from one end and the second 1 cm/½ in from the first hole.

9 Drill the holes using a drill bit the same size as the copper tube. Use a hacksaw to cut two lengths of copper tube. Use the long-nosed pliers to bend one end of each copper tube into a hook shape. Use the chrome rail to estimate the curve of the hooks. Each hook should fit snugly around the chrome rail with its end fitting into the drilled hole.

▶

10 Position the shower rail sockets on the wall so that the rails slot into them. Use a spirit level (carpenter's level) to check that the outer two are level.

11 Refer to the diagram below. Push the chrome rails through the holes in the back of the canopy, then fit the copper tubes in place to hold the front section rigid. Fit the straight end of each copper tube into the hole in each side rail. Fit the hooked ends over the middle rail and into the two drilled holes. Fix a row of cup hooks to the ceiling directly above the front edge of the canopy. Loop white cord around the cup hooks and the chrome rails for added stability. Finally, cap the chrome pipe with copper caps.

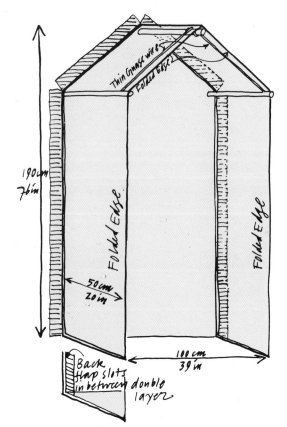

DETAILS

"Everything there is simply

order and beauty"

CHARLES BAUDELAIRE

Introduction

"The pleasure of what we enjoy
is lost by coveting more"
ENGLISH PROVERB

Small is beautiful, and it is often the accessories in a room that can have the most impact. A vase of flowers, cushions and lampshades give a room a cosy, cared-for feel. Lighting can completely change the character of a room – aim for several strategically placed lamps instead of one central light. Lampshades make inexpensive canvases for trying out new decorative techniques.

In the kitchen, make use of shelves, baskets and wire holders to create a room of individuality rather than a blank, fitted space. Take another look at everyday objects, such as terracotta pots, baby-carrying baskets and roof flashing, for inspiration.

Above: A selection of tin containers provides the backdrop to an arrangement of dried plant materials.

shelves

baskets

wire containers

lampshades

Above and left: Ribbons and whimsical decoration can be used sparingly to great effect.

Above: A simple wire container holds bathroom essentials.

*Above and right: The use of natural materials is a striking feature
of the pared-down interior.*

FRINGED SHELF EDGING

The simplest and most inexpensive shelving assumes designer status when adorned with a frivolous skirt of raffia. You can adapt the technique to suit deeper shelving, either by plaiting (braiding) with more strands of raffia or by using thick rope instead. If you are using rope, fray the ends to produce the fringed effect. You can trim the ends for a neat finish or leave them irregular for a natural look.

YOU WILL NEED
raffia
shelf
large rubber band
scissors
drawing pins (thumbtacks) or double-sided tape

1 Bunch together 60 strands of raffia about 1½ times as long as the shelf to be edged. Attach one end to a door handle or nail using a rubber band.

2 Divide the raffia into three groups of 20 strands and begin to plait (braid).

3 To produce a flat plait, keep your thumbs on top of the raffia as you work. Turning your thumbs towards the centre would produce a round cord.

4 Cut some shorter pieces of raffia and group them in bunches of ten. Fold the first group of ten in half to form a loop. Push this loop through one of the loops in the plait.

5 Pull the loose ends through the loop to form a knot. Add bunches of raffia along the whole length of the plait in the same way. Trim the ends to make an even fringe if desired.

6 Finally, attach the shelf edging to the shelf using drawing pins (thumbtacks) or double-sided tape.

Right: Fringed raffia adds a quirky touch to an otherwise unadorned interior.

WAVY SHELF EDGING AND FRAMES

Corrugated paper is an undervalued material that can look absolutely stunning if used imaginatively. It is easy to work with and has many uses. Experiment with different shapes to see which looks most pleasing. Bear in mind, however, that corrugated paper crushes very easily so, before starting work, flatten it with a ruler. It will still look ridged but won't mark. Coloured corrugated paper is available from art shops.

YOU WILL NEED

tape measure

roll of natural corrugated paper

scissors

ruler

thin cardboard

pencil

craft knife

cutting mat

spray adhesive

masking tape (optional)

fine corrugated paper in different colours

paper glue

1 Measure the width of the windowsill or shelf and cut the corrugated paper to this measurement, plus the required drop. Flatten the ridges with a ruler.

2 Draw the design on to cardboard and cut out to use as a template. Draw the shape on the natural corrugated paper, using the template. Cut it out with a craft knife on a cutting mat.

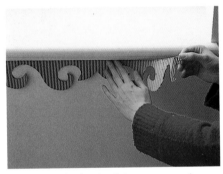

3 Spray the back of the corrugated paper with adhesive and fix in position. If you want to remove the decoration later, stick masking tape under the windowsill and glue the decoration to the tape. You can peel off the tape without harming the wall.

4 To make a picture frame, measure the image that will be framed and decide on the size and shape required. Draw the frame backing on to corrugated paper and cut it out with the craft knife and ruler.

5 Use the backing as a template to draw and cut out the front of the frame from coloured corrugated paper. Cut out the central frame area.

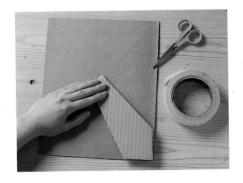

6 Stick the image in position with paper glue so the backing colour shows through, forming a narrow border all round. Make a stand for the frame with a piece of corrugated paper cut to the shape shown.

Right: Complete the look with decorative covers for candles and books.

PEWTER-LOOK SHELF

Aluminium flashing, traditionally used in roofing, takes on an unusual, pitted appearance that resembles pewter when it is hammered. It can be used to cover simple shapes such as this shelf, and it is very difficult to guess what the original material is. Practise your hammering technique on a scrap of flashing first to achieve the right texture, and use a ball hammer to make smooth, regular indentations.

YOU WILL NEED
sheet of 18 mm/¾ in MDF (medium-density fiberboard)
pencil
ruler
handsaw
drill and drill bit
wood glue
2 screws
screwdriver
aluminium flashing
craft knife
ball hammer

1 Enlarge the template at the back of the book. Using it as a guide, mark the two shelf pieces on MDF (medium-density fiberboard). Cut them out. Draw a line down the centre and mark two points for the drill holes. Mark corresponding points on the long edge of the stand. Drill holes at these points. Glue and screw the shelf and stand together.

2 Cut lengths of aluminium flashing roughly to size. Peel away the backing and stick them to the shelf front, trimming the rough edges on the side of the strips as you go.

3 Butt each new length of flashing very closely to the last, so that no MDF is visible beneath the covering.

4 When the front is covered, lay the shelf face down and trim away the excess flashing using a craft knife.

5 With a craft knife, cut lengths of flashing to cover the back and sides of the shelf, and stick them in place.

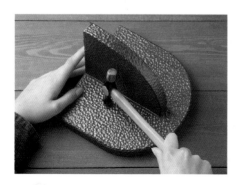

6 Using a ball hammer, tap the surface of the flashing to make indentations close together. Vary the force with which you strike the flashing, so as to make an interesting and irregular pattern.

Right: The simple design of the shelf is enhanced by the textured "pewter" effect.

WALL SCONCE

This simple, elegant sconce is made from small, fluted cake moulds. The shiny rippled surfaces reflect and intensify the candlelight beautifully. Catering suppliers stock all sorts of interesting moulds for confectionery and cakes. The moulds are very simply joined using fine wire and pop rivets and a wire loop is added to suspend the sconce from the wall. Never leave nightlights and candles unattended.

YOU WILL NEED
protective clothing and gloves
30 gauge/0.01 in tin plate
scallop mould and oval mould
tin shears
pliers
file
wooden block
drill and drill bit
pop riveter and rivets
felt-tipped pen
bradawl
fine wire
wire-cutters
round-nosed pliers

1 Wearing protective clothing and gloves, cut a 20 cm/8 in strip of tin about 7 mm/¼ in wider than the base of the scallop mould. Carefully turn over and flatten the long sides of the strip using pliers. File the corners smooth.

2 Place the tin strip on a block of wood. Hold the edge with pliers and drill two holes in one end of the strip. File the holes smooth. Bend forward the lip of the scallop mould using pliers. Place the tin strip on the lip and mark where the holes are. Drill holes in the mould and file down any rough edges.

3 Line up the holes in the mould and the tin strip and pop rivet the two together. Using pliers, bend the tin strip down, then outwards to make a shelf. Hold the oval mould on the block of wood with pliers and drill two holes in the bottom. File the holes smooth.

4 Place the mould on the shelf and mark where the edge of the mould comes to and the position of the holes. Drill two holes in the shelf and file the edges smooth. Cut off the excess tin strip and file the edge smooth. Pop rivet the mould to the shelf.

5 Pierce two holes in the back of the sconce. File the holes smooth. To make a hanger, cut a length of fine wire, make a coil in one end, then pass the uncoiled end through the sconce. Make a loop, then pass the wire back through.

PIN-PRICKED LAMPSHADE

This simple but impressive technique is most effective on a neutral coloured paper shade with a smooth surface, so avoid dark colours. The shell motif evokes memories of summer days and shoreline walks,* perfect for lighting up dark winter evenings. When the lamp is lit, the pattern glows and makes a real focal point for the room. Do not use this technique on a fabric or a fabric-covered shade.

YOU WILL NEED
tracing paper
soft and hard pencils
white paper
scissors
masking tape
paper lampshade
towel
heavy-duty darning needle
thimble
heavy cartridge paper (optional)

1 Trace the template at the back of the book and enlarge if necessary. Copy it several times. Cut out the motifs roughly.

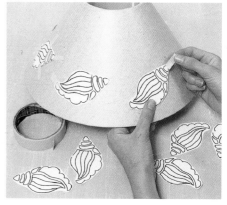

2 Use masking tape to fix the motifs in a pattern all round the shade to provide positioning guides. Here, the motifs were positioned around the border, but an all-over pattern would work equally well.

3 Transfer the motif on to tracing paper and rub over the reverse with a soft pencil. Trace the motif on the inside of the shade, following the positioning guides. Draw on any extra patterning. Remove the copies from the outside.

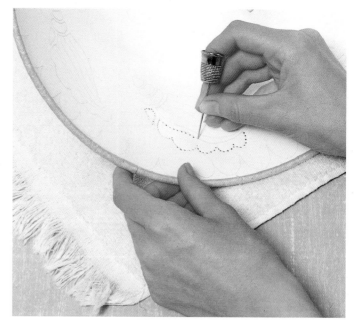

4 Resting the shade on a towel, prick out the motif from the wrong side, so that tiny bumps appear on the surface. You may practise on heavy cartridge paper first, to get the right feel and to check that the motif is suitable.

PEBBLE LAMPSHADE

Bring a touch of class and a quirky seaside style to a simple brown paper lampshade. Using pebbles worn smooth by sea water and picked up at the beach, you can create a work of art that is truly individual. All natural materials work harmoniously together, so pebbles and raffia combined with brown paper are absolutely perfect. An alternative idea would be to bind the metal stem with string to add to the natural feel.

YOU WILL NEED
raffia
paper lampshade with perforated edge
hole punch (optional)
small pebbles
glue gun
scissors

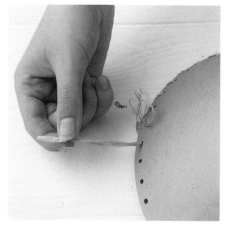

1 Thread the raffia through the top and bottom edges of the lampshade. If the shade does not have perforations, punch a row of evenly spaced holes.

2 Pull thin strips of raffia apart and position the pieces on the pebbles. Glue them in place with a glue gun, and leave to set for a few seconds.

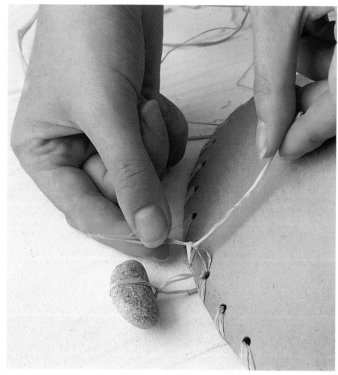

3 Tie the lengths of raffia around each pebble in neat knots.

4 Hang the stones all around the lampshade, knotting the pebbles in place. Trim the loose ends of the raffia.

SCALLOPED TABLECLOTH

A plastic tablecloth is invaluable on a table that gets a lot of use, as it can be wiped clean in seconds. To make it attractive as well as practical, cut a shaped trim and make a design along the edge using a hole punch. Add ribbon or cord in a contrasting colour for extra visual and textural appeal.

YOU WILL NEED
tape measure
plastic-coated fabric
pencil
dressmaker's scissors
cardboard
circular object, such as a jar lid (optional)
scissors
hole punch
ribbon, string or rope (optional)

1 Measure your table and cut the fabric to the required size. Draw a scallop shape on to cardboard, tracing round a circular object if necessary, and cut out. Draw around the template on the wrong side of the plastic fabric.

2 Cut the edging shape with sharp dressmaker's scissors, keeping the lines smooth and fluid.

3 Punch out a design with a hole punch. You could thread ribbon, string or fine cord through the holes to add even more interest.

TEXTURED TABLECLOTH

A mass of trimmings is now available, and a trip around the haberdashery (notions) department will, with a little imagination, generate any number of ideas. Here, simple upholsterer's webbing was used to edge a tablecloth. The webbing was decorated with string in very loose loops.

YOU WILL NEED
about 2 m/2¼ yd hessian (burlap)
dressmaker's scissors
dressmaker's pins
needle and tacking (basting) thread
iron
sewing machine
matching sewing thread
8 m/8¾ yd webbing
brown string

1 Cut the hessian (burlap) to the size of the tablecloth you require, allowing for hems. Turn under the hems and pin, tack (baste), press and machine stitch. Cut a length of webbing to go round all four sides. Pin and machine stitch the webbing around the edge.

2 Lay the string on the webbing and experiment by twisting it into different designs.

3 Pin, tack and hand stitch the string to the webbing, to hold it securely. It doesn't matter if there are gaps in the stitching; the looseness of the string is all part of the effect.

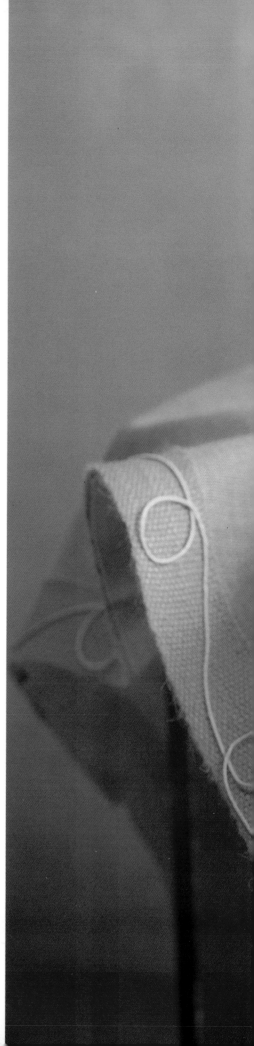

SEASIDE SHOWER CURTAIN

Give your shower room a feel of the great outdoors with this refreshing scene of starfish, shells and seaweed swaying gently. The clear shower curtain provides a watery backdrop for you to create your very own seaside mood with whatever marine motifs you choose. The example shown here uses a monochromatic crisp white scheme, but it could work equally well with warm, bright colours.

YOU WILL NEED
pencil
paper
scissors
clear plastic shower curtain
masking tape
white waterproof paint
fine paintbrush

1 Trace the templates from the back of the book.

2 Reduce or enlarge the images as needed to fit your chosen design for the shower curtain.

3 Cut out the paper templates or designs and arrange them on the shower curtain.

4 Position the paper templates on a large tabletop in the desired pattern and secure them in place with masking tape. Use a table with a tough surface that will not be harmed by the tape.

5 Place the shower curtain on top of the images and tape it down firmly. Using white waterproof paint and a fine paintbrush, carefully paint the images on to the shower curtain surface. Leave it to dry thoroughly before hanging up.

UTILITY RACK

The shelf at the bottom of this useful and simply designed rack is wide enough to hold four food cans. Stripped of their labels, the cans make attractive storage containers that complement the rack. Alternatively, the shelf will hold three small plant pots. Screwed to the wall, it will be quite secure and capable of holding a considerable weight. The little basket at the bottom is made from a small sieve.

YOU WILL NEED
straining wire
ruler
permanent marker pen
round-nosed pliers
galvanized wire 1.65 mm/0.065 in and 0.65 mm/0.025 in thick
general-purpose pliers
small-gauge chicken wire
gloves

diagram 1

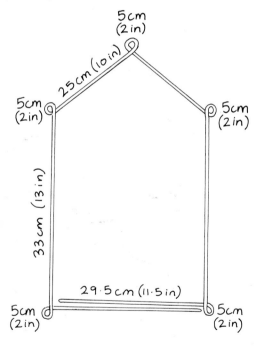

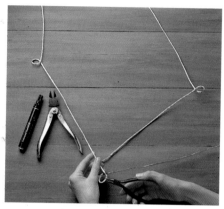

1 To make the frame, cut a 2 m/79 in length of straining wire. Twist the ends tightly to stop them unravelling and, with permanent marker pen, mark the wire at intervals of 29.5 cm/11½ in, 5 cm/2 in, 33 cm/13 in, 5 cm/2 in, 25 cm/10 in, 5 cm/2 in, 25 cm/10 in, 5 cm/2 in, 33 cm/13 in, 5 cm/2 in and 29.5 cm/11½ in. Using round-nosed pliers, make a loop with each 5 cm/2 in section, making sure that the pen marks match up and that all the loops face outwards (see diagram 1).

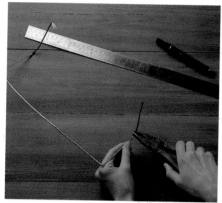

2 Using the 0.65 mm/0.025 in galvanized wire, bind the two 29.5 cm/11½ in sections together to make the bottom of the frame. To make the shelf, cut a 72 cm/29 in length of straining wire and mark it at intervals of 2 cm/1 in, 9 cm/3½ in, 10 cm/4 in, 30 cm/12 in, 10 cm/4 in, 9 cm/3½ in and 2 cm/1 in. Using general-purpose pliers, bend the wire at right angles at these points (see diagram 2).

diagram 2

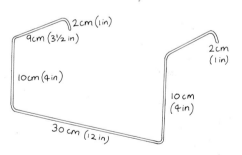

3 Mark each side of the frame 10 cm/4 in from the bottom. Twist the 2 cm/1 in ends of the straining wire tightly around the frame at these points.

▶

4 To make the rim and sides of the shelf, cut a 104 cm/41½ in length of 1.65 mm/ 0.065 in galvanized wire and mark it at intervals of 2 cm/1 in, 13 cm/ 5 in, 9 cm/3½ in, 13 cm/5 in, 30 cm/ 12 in, 13 cm/5 in, 9 cm/3½ in, 13 cm/ 5 in and 2 cm/1 in. Using round-nosed pliers, make a loop with the 2 cm/1 in section at each end of the wire. Bend the wire at the 13 cm/5 in and 9 cm/3½ in points at 45° angles to form the side crosses of the shelf. Bend the 30 cm/ 12 in section in the middle at right angles to form the top rim (see diagram 3).

5 Tack (baste) the loops at the ends of the rim wire to the 10 cm/4 in markings on the sides of the main frame. Tack each corner of the side crosses to the frame (see diagram 4).

diagram 4

6 Wearing gloves for protection, lay the frame on to the flat piece of chicken wire and cut around the frame. Allow 30 cm/12 in at the bottom for wrapping around the shelf, so that there is a double thickness of chicken wire at the front of the shelf where it tucks inside. Using 0.65 mm/0.025 in galvanized wire, bind the edges of the chicken wire to the frame. Wrap any rough edges at the top around the frame before binding. Bind the shelf firmly to the frame as you bind on the chicken wire and remove the tacking wire.

diagram 3

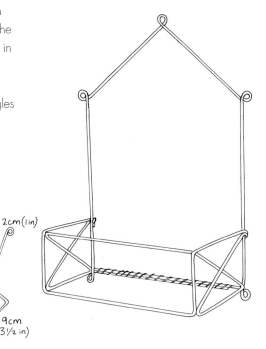

Above: The chicken wire adds a decorative quality to the practical nature of the shelf.

WIRE EGG TREE

The design for this whimsical egg tree derives from Eastern European folk art. The basket at the bottom is traditionally used for bread. The tree makes a spectacular centrepiece at Easter when filled with dyed or painted eggs. Tinned copper wire has been used here as it is ideal for kitchenware. It is as malleable as copper wire and has the added advantage that it does not tarnish.

YOU WILL NEED
tinned copper wire 2 mm/0.078 in and
1 mm/0.039 in thick
ruler
permanent marker pen
rolling pin
large egg
wire-cutters
general-purpose pliers
pencil
strong tape

1 Measure 60 cm/24 in of 2 mm/ 0.078 in tinned copper wire, but do not cut off. Mark the point and wrap this section of wire three times around the rolling pin. Remove and grip the middle of the final loop between your thumb and forefinger. Wrap the loop around your thumb and pull it down. The second loop should now be reduced in diameter. These three loops form the egg holder. Refine the shape by moulding it around a large egg.

2 Bend the remaining end of wire up the outside of the egg holder to meet the wire still attached to the spool. Bend both wires away from the egg holder to make the branch.

3 Bind the two branch wires together using 8 cm/3¼ in of 1 mm/0.039 in wire. Bend the wires down at a right angle. Leave an allowance of 2 cm/1 in, then cut off the end. Measure 60 cm/ 24 in, then cut off the wire from the spool. Make ten more egg holders in this way. The section of six lower holders measures 8 cm/3¼ in, and the section for the five upper holders measures 4 cm/1½ in.

4 Measure 5 cm/2 in of 2 mm/ 0.078 in wire and mark the point. Wrap the next section ten times around a pencil to form petals. Bend the petals round to form a flower. Use the first 5 cm/ 2 in of wire to join the flower together and cut off. Bend the remaining wire down from the flower at a right angle to make the stem. Cut off at 75 cm/30 in.

5 Form the top egg holder as described in step one, but this time wrap the first loop around your thumb and pull down. Measure 70 cm/27½ in and cut off the wire from the spool.

▶

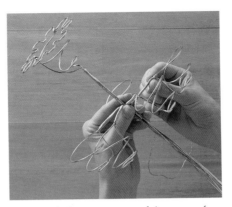

6 Bind the end of the top egg holder on to the flower opposite the join. To hold the wires in place while you are working, bind them together with tacking wire. Bend the long wire extending from the flower to curve down the outside of the spiral. Using 1 mm/0.039 in wire, start binding the two stems tightly together. Bind for 7 cm/2¾ in.

7 Bunch the stem wires of the upper five egg holders around the two stem wires to form the trunk. Wrap with a piece of strong tape to keep them in place. Using 1 mm/0.039 in wire, start binding the trunk from just below the point where the egg holders join the stem. Bind the trunk for 7 cm/2¾ in. Then bind on the six lower egg holders in the same way. Bind the trunk for approximately 25 cm/10 in below this second tier.

8 To make the basket, cut six lengths of 2 mm/0.078 in wire measuring 90 cm/36 in, 89 cm/35½ in, 88 cm/35 in, 75 cm/30 in, 65 cm/26 in and 46 cm/18 in. Bend hooks at the ends of the wires and close up to make six rings. Squeeze the hooks tightly closed.

9 Splay out the wires from the base of the egg tree and curve upwards to form the side struts of the basket. Check that the diameter at the top is the same as that of the largest ring.

10 Tack (baste) the rings on to the struts, starting with the smallest at the bottom and working up to the largest at the top. Allow 2.5 cm/1 in between each ring. Attach the largest ring by wrapping the ends of the strut wires around it. The basket should be approximately 9 cm/3½ in in height. Bind the rings on to the struts.

"ANTIQUE" TERRACOTTA POT

Laundry in a flowerpot? It sounds unusual, but this idea makes a refreshing change from wicker baskets in the bathroom. Terracotta pots are now available in a huge range of shapes and sizes and a visit to your local garden centre should provide you with just the right pot. This technique gives the pristine pot an antique feel.

YOU WILL NEED
old rag
shellac button polish
large terracotta flowerpot
white emulsion (latex) paint
paintbrushes
scouring pad
sandpaper (optional)

1 Soak a rag in shellac button polish and rub the surface of the terracotta pot with it. The polish will sink in very fast, leaving a yellow sheen.

2 Mix equal quantities of white paint with water. Stir it well and apply a coat to the pot. Allow to dry.

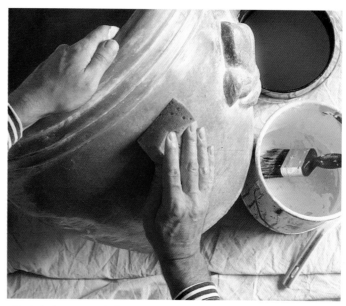

3 Rub the pot with the scouring pad to remove most of the white paint. The paint will cling to the crevices and along the mouldings to look like limescale. Either leave the pot like this or rub it back further with sandpaper to reveal the clay. When you are happy with the effect, apply a coat of button polish with a brush to seal the surface.

BASKET STORAGE

These generous-sized Moses baskets were designed to transport babies in great comfort. Sadly, they do not conform to any safety regulations so present-day newborns have safe plastic and metal carriers instead. Moses baskets are used here as fresh and airy containers for clothes, such as socks and underwear.

YOU WILL NEED
plank of wood
tape measure
saw
medium-grade sandpaper
drill, with wood and masonry bits
1 long or 2 short branches (or dowels)
penknife (or wood carving knife)
dowel (optional)
2 Moses baskets
wood glue
hammer
wallplugs and screws
screwdriver

1 Cut two squares of wood at least 12 x 12 cm/4¾ x 4¾ in and 5 cm/2 in deep. Sand the edges and drill a hole through the middle of each square, slightly smaller than the diameter of the branches. Carve away the branch ends so that they fit tightly into the holes. Sand it slightly.

2 Use scraps from the branches or pieces of dowel for the pegs. Taper the ends.

3 Measure the distance between the basket handles and drill two holes that far apart on top of each branch. The holes should fit the pegs correctly. Apply wood glue to each branch and tap them into each square, making sure that the pegs are on top. Apply wood glue to the peg ends and fit them into each branch. To fix the top branch to the wall, drill holes in the four corners of the square of wood, and four corresponding holes in the wall. Using the wallplugs and screws, screw the branch to the wall. Fix the lower branch to the wall allowing about 10 cm/4 in clearance from the top basket.

Templates

To enlarge the templates to the correct size, use either a grid system or a photocopier. For the grid system, trace the template and draw a grid of evenly spaced squares over your tracing. To scale up, draw a larger grid on to another piece of paper. Copy the outline on to the the second grid by taking each square individually and drawing the relevant part of the outline in the larger square. Finally, draw over the lines to make sure they are continuous.

pp52-53 Embroidered Pillowcase

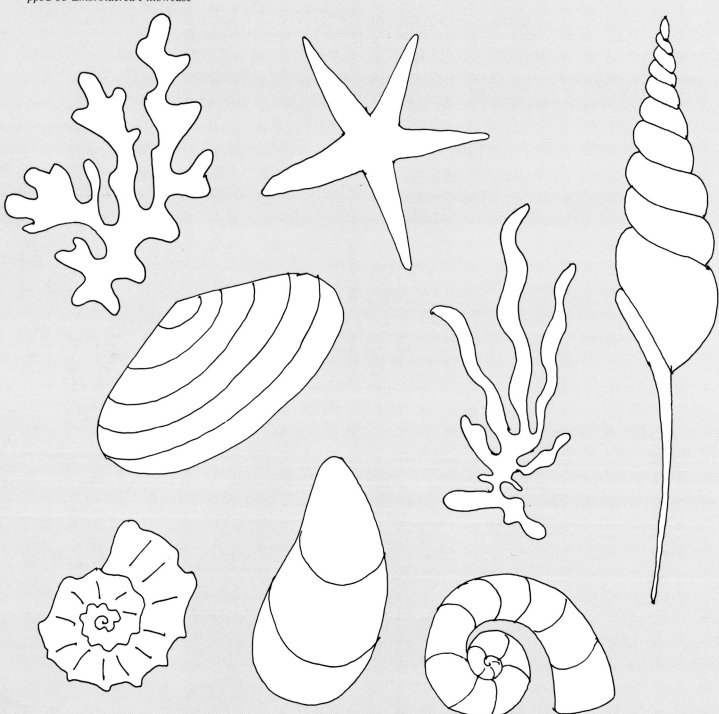

pp132-133 Pewter-look Shelf

pp144-145 Seaside Shower Curtain

pp136-137 Pin-pricked Lampshade

pp114-115 Stamped Shelf

ACKNOWLEDGEMENTS

The publishers would like to thank the following for designing the projects in this book.

Deena Beverley: Stringwork Curtains; Rope-wrapped Chair
Penny Boylon: Pin-pricked Lampshade
Marion Elliot: Pewter-look Shelf; Wall Sconce
Andrew Gilmore: Scallop-hinged Cupboard; Wire Egg Tree
Mary Maguire: Utility Rack
Andrea Spencer: Shell Shocked; Striped Hanging; Cushioned Comfort; Embroidered Pillowcases; Lovely Linens; Sheer Magic; Rough Plaster Wall; Crackle Glaze Shutters; Washed Floorboards; Pebble Dash Paving; Slatted Decking; Rope-trimmed Sofa; Packing Crate Shelves; Hanging Shelves; Wooden Headboard; Fringed Shelf Edging; Corrugated Shelf Edging and Frames;
Pebble Lampshade; Scalloped Tablecloth; Textured Tablecloth; Seaside Shower Curtain
Judy Smith: Tuscan Doorway; Stamped Wall Panels; Paper Panels; Rope Decoration;
Catherine Tully: Romantic Chair Cover; Gilded Chair;
Stewart and Sally Walton: Muslin Curtains; Cotton Fresh; Fabric-swathed Chair; Lace-trimmed Bedlinen; Japanese Futon; Woodland Stripes; Cork-stamped Floorboards; Bucket Stool; Stamped Shelf; Twig Headboard; Calico Canopy; "Antique" Terracotta Pot; Moses Basket

PICTURE CREDITS

Michelle Garrett: pages 8 (top and second from top); 10br; 12bl; 14tl; 14br; 15 (second from top); 15br; 16; 17; 18bl; 19br; 24b; 29bl; 29br; 29tl; 94bl; 95bl; 95tr; 124; 126bl; 126tr; 127t

Tim Imrie: pages 21r; 27br; 31; 62-63

Debbie Patterson: pages 11bl; 12br; 13bl; 13br; 22b; 23bl 25b; 125; 137

Spike Powell: pages 8bl; 8 (third from top); 10bl; 12 tr; 25tl; 27bl; 28tr; 32t; 33b; 44-45; 52-53; 67tl; 67tr; 68-69; 82-89; 94tr; 94br; 95tl; 110-113; 118-119; 127bl; 138-139; 144-145

Graham Rae: pages 9; 10tr; 11 tr; 20br; 21tl; 21bl; 23cr; 24t; 27tr; 29tl; 32b; 36-43; 46-51; 54-61; 65; 66tr; 66br; 67b; 70-81; 90-91; 92-93; 95br; 99-105; 114-117; 120-123; 128-131; 140-143; 152-155

Peter Williams: pages 8br; 15 (third from top); 19bl; 20bl; 20c; 21cl; 26; 27tr; 23br; 30; 33t; 34-35; 96-98; 106-109; 127br; 132-135; 146-151

Polly Wreford: pages 14br; 15bl; 15tr; 18c; 20t; 23tr; 28bl; 64; 66bl; 126br

INDEX